MODELLING MODERN
SOVIET FIGHTER AIRCRAFT

MODELLING MODERN SOVIET FIGHTER AIRCRAFT

Ken Duffey

ARGUS BOOKS

Argus Books
Argus House
Boundary Way
Hemel Hempstead
Hertfordshire HP2 7ST
England

First published by Argus Books 1990

ISBN 1 85486 034 8

Phototypesetting by Photoprint, Torquay, Devon
Printed and bound in Great Britain by Dotesios Printers Ltd, Trowbridge, Wilts.

CONTENTS

ACKNOWLEDGEMENTS

Kelvin Barber and Ken Jones for their encouragement; Tim Perry for the model photographs; John Lewis for the missile drawings; Pat Shearing for some of the typing; and finally my two young daughters, Alex and Michelle, for putting up with the chaos in the house while I was writing this book.

1 INTRODUCTION

'The Russians are coming!, the Russians are coming!' The title of the 1966 Alan Arkin comedy film could be used to describe the current spate of kit releases of Soviet warplanes and the increasing interest in this subject among modellers worldwide.

There was a time, not too many years ago, when anyone interested in Soviet aircraft had to make do with totally inaccurate kits and a scarcity of information on which to attempt scratch-building. However, in the last couple of years, and especially since the new 'openness' in Soviet society, the number of available kits has multiplied as manufacturers strive to find new avenues and subjects on which to apply their kit-producing skills, and more data becomes available to enable them to do so. Indeed, there is now so much openness that it is easier to obtain details of the cockpit of the very latest Soviet warplane – the SU–27 Flanker – than it is to get a shot of the interior of the now obsolete TU–28P Fiddler!

Nonetheless, all is not yet perfect for the Soviet aircraft modeller, for, in their eagerness to be first with a new kit, some manufacturers jump the gun and base their models on the earliest available data, with the result that their kits are inaccurate and the investment needed to correct them in the light of later information is too prohibitive for them to contemplate. Witness Hasegawa's MiG–29 Fulcrum and Revell's SU–27 Flanker – both kits were produced using insufficient information with the result that both kits are wide of the mark.

For anyone contemplating modelling Soviet types, I recommend that they join a modelling club or society where they can 'pick the brains' of fellow members and talk to like-minded modellers to swap ideas and information. Certainly to be recommended is the International Plastic Modelling Society (IPMS) which has a special Soviet section or Special Interest Group (SIG). The addresses of both are listed in Appendix I.

Another valuable source of information is the pen-friend – especially from the Soviet-bloc countries – many of whom have access to local aviation magazines and data. Requests for pen-friendships appear regularly in modelling magazines such as *Scale Models International* and *Fine Scale Modeler*.

I hope this book will inspire you to have a go at a Soviet aircraft model – they certainly generate a great deal of interest at model shows and make a change from all those Phantoms, Eagles and Fighting Falcons!

Ken Duffey
March 1990

2 SOVIET ORGANIZATION

There is no Soviet Air Force, as such. The organization is made up of a number of elements under the encompassing title of The Air Forces of the USSR or VOENNO-VOZDUSHNIYE SILY (V-VS) which covers all the activities from close air support to the operation of the Strategic ICBM force.

The principal components of the V-VS are the Air Forces of the Anti-aircraft Defence of the Homeland or PROTIVO – VOZDUSH-NAYA OBORONA (STRANY) (P-VO STRANY), the Long Range Aviation or DAL'NAYA AVIATSIYA (DA), the Frontal Aviation or FRONTOVAYA AVIATISIYA (FA), the Transport Aviation or VOENNO-TRANSPORTNAYA AVIATSIYA (V-TA) and the Naval Air Force or AVIATSIYA VOENNO-MORSKOVA FLOTA (AV-MF).

The P-VO STRANY is responsible for all of the air defence of the USSR, and operates anti-aircraft artillery, surface-to-air missiles, ground-based and airborne early warning radars, as well as the manned interceptor force, the ISTREBITEL'NAYA AVIATSIYA P-VO STRANY or IA P-VO STRANY. Its nearest conceptual equivalent would be the United States Air Defence Command and it operates such types as the Fiddler, Foxbat and Firebar, all of which are being replaced by the much more potent Foxhounds, Fulcrums and Flankers.

The Soviet equivalent of the US Strategic Air Command is the DA, which operates the bomber types (not covered by this book), while the V-TA has a similar role to the American Military Airlift Command.

The USA's Tactical Air Command is paralleled by the Soviet Frontal Aviation which operates in concert with the ground forces with close air-support, tactical strike and reconnaissance, etc., as part of its repertoire. It is this element which operates the MiG–27 Flogger-D, SU–7/22 Fitter and SU–25 Frogfoot, among others, as well as the longer-range SU–24 Fencer.

Naval Aviation, AV-MF, operates a number of bomber types in the anti-ship role as well as the amphibious BE–12 Mail flying-boat and various anti-submarine helicopters. Its only current fighter type, carried by the anti-submarine carriers of the Kiev class, is the

Yak-38 Forger V/STOL aircraft, although, with the entry into service of the new Tblisi class of aircraft carrier, such types as navalised versions of the Flanker, Fulcrum and Frogfoot may well enter the inventory.

3 NATO REPORTING NAMES

Because of the reticence of the Soviets to reveal information about new aircraft types, and the confusing array of type numbers allocated by the individual design bureaux OPYTNO KONSTRUK-TORSKOYE BYURO (OKB) and the Service designations, the Air Standards Co-ordinating Committee (ASCC) of NATO decided to adopt a new identification system in 1954 to allocate reporting names to Soviet aircraft.

This system consists of a simple key, whereby bombers and attack aircraft are allocated reporting names beginning with the letter 'B' indicating Bomber. Fighters and fighter-bombers commence with the letter 'F' for Fighter. Transports, both civil and military, start with 'C' for Cargo, and all other types of fixed-wing aircraft (e.g. trainers, flying-boats, tankers etc.) have reporting names beginning with the letter 'M' for Miscellaneous.

To differentiate between airscrew-driven and turbojet-driven aircraft, the latter's reporting names consist of two syllables while the former has only one. Thus BEAR is a propeller-driven bomber while BLACKJACK is a turbojet/turbofan-powered bomber. Similarly, FRED was allocated to the Bell P–63 Kingcobra, which was supplied to the USSR under Lend-Lease during WW2, while FLANKER is the appellation applied to the latest Soviet jet interceptor, the SU–27.

All rotorcraft, whether piston-engined or turboshaft-powered, are given names beginning with 'H' for Helicopter and there is no significance in the number of syllables. For instance, HIND and HORMONE are both turboshaft-powered types.

Soviet missiles are also given NATO designations and reporting names. Air-to-air types are allocated names beginning with the letter 'A' while air-to-surface weapons have names starting with the letter 'K'. Thus, the long-range R–27 AAM which arms the Flanker is designated AA–10 Alamo by NATO, while the air-to-ground Soviet equivalent of the American Bullpup, which is carried by such types as the Forger and Fitter, is given the name AS–7 Kerry.

4 GENERAL HINTS

COLOURS AND MARKINGS

Until recently, most Soviet fighters were unpainted and left in bare metal. This finish is very difficult to achieve on a model and various publications recommend different methods, from the use of silver foil cut to the shape of the various panels, to a kind of silver paste which is applied to the model and then 'buffed up'.

A range of metal-finish paints has been released by Humbrol under the name Metalcote, with Polished Aluminium, Matt Aluminium and Polished Steel being particularly appropriate. These are best airbrushed onto the model in different combinations and they can then be polished to give a varying degree of shine to represent the panels. Although this can be quite effective, I have found that the best method of representing bare metal is to apply Humbrol's Polished Aluminium overall and, when dry, to cover it with an airbrushed coat of SNJ Spray Metal. This is a fairly new product from the USA which can only be sprayed on, can be masked without the paint lifting when the mask is removed, and can be painted over with other colours.

Some air-defence fighters, such as late MiG–21s, MiG–23s and the MiG–25 Foxbat, are finished in an overall light grey scheme while ground-attack types – the MiG–27, SU–22 and SU–25 are camouflaged in a disruptive pattern of greens, browns and tans. The two latest Soviet types, the MiG–29 Fulcrum and the SU–27 Flanker, although fulfilling the same basic interceptor role, sport different colour schemes – greens and greys for the former and blues and greys on the latter.

While exact colour matches obviously cannot be given, most kit manufacturers include a drawing of the relevant scheme and quote paint numbers – usually their own brand. Not all of these quoted schemes are correct, however, a classic example being Revell who show their Flanker in a light olive green and blue-grey finish. So it pays to cross-check as many references as possible and try to arrive at a reasonably accurate colour match – after all no-one can argue too strongly that your scheme is wrong!

If, like me, you are not an expert at airbrushing, the following tip given to me by a fellow modeller may prove useful. To get a nice soft edge to a camouflage pattern, first airbrush the lightest colour over the whole upper surface and, when this is dry, lay Blu-Tack, rolled into string-like lengths, over the upper surfaces in the camouflage pattern, where the colours meet. The Blu-Tack will adhere to the model without marring the surface. Then mask the lighter areas with Maskol or masking tape and airbrush the model with the darker colour. When the paint is dry and all the masking and Blu-Tack is removed, the camouflage will be soft-edged where the Blu-Tack has acted like a raised mask.

Radomes and dielectric panels are usually in dark grey or mid-green, and the cockpit colours are, generally, light blue-green side-walls and instrument panel, with black instrument faces. Seats are usually grey or black with green or grey cushions and dark blue straps. Undercarriage legs are either light grey or green, and the wheel hubs are usually dark green.

Soviet markings consist of a five-pointed red star with a white outline and red border, applied in six positions, on upper and lower surfaces of both wings and on the vertical fin. The star on the fin has one arm pointing upwards and the flat top on the side arms parallel with the fuselage datum, while the wing stars have one arm pointing forward and the flat top of the side arms at right-angles to the fuselage centreline. Apart from the mass of stencilling applied to the airframe, the only other marking regularly seen is a two-digit code number, usually in blue, red or yellow with a thin black outline, applied to the nose below the cockpit or on the intake trunking.

Some aircraft, particularly those participating at Western air-shows, have sported the OKB's house logo. Both MiG and Sukhoi types at Paris had a manufacturer's symbol adorning the aircraft – in two completely different styles, in the case of the Sukhoi bureau.

Finally on the subject of markings, I must mention the 'Out-standing Unit' award which is sometimes seen on Soviet aircraft. This consists of a stylised aircraft with a contrail passing through a pentagon and is usually applied to the nose area. A fine example of this marking was to be found on Hasegawa's MiG–23 Flogger but, sadly, this has disappeared from the re-release.

ACCESSORIES

The Soviet aircraft modeller is reasonably well catered for by the cottage-industry manufacturers who provide a whole range of accessories with which to enhance the finished kit.

Decals of Soviet stars and numerals can be obtained from the specialist decal manufacturers, particularly the US firms of Superscale (formerly Microscale) and Scalemaster. Superscale supply a sheet of different sized stars in red with white and yellow borders plus a sheet of numerals in different colours and styles, and the Scalemaster sheet SM–34 contains a host of different sized red stars and intake warning triangles. These sheets are a must for the modeller, as some of the earlier kits, especially the vacforms, do not have any Soviet markings included.

The ejection seats included in most kits bear little resemblance to the real thing, and are very crude representations. Most look at though they would be at home in my front lounge doubling as armchairs, and they should be replaced.

Aeroclub provide a number of white-metal ejection seats to fit Soviet aircraft types. Included in the range are examples for the MiG–15, MiG–17, MiG–21F/PF, MiG–29 and SU–25. As well as replacing the kit items, white-metal seats have the added advantage of providing an ideal nose weight to prevent the model becoming a tail-sitter.

Aeroclub also provide replacement vacformed canopies for the Fagot, Fresco, Farmer, Fishbed and Fitter. The latter can also be used on the Flagon and Fishpot. Also in their range are conversion kits for the MiG–17. These are designed to complement the KP kit and comprise new vacformed fuselages, metal intake rings and jetpipes and canopies for the Fresco-A, -C and -D.

PP Aeroparts also include a Soviet seat in their range. This is a super-detailed white-metal KM–1 ejection seat as fitted to later MiG–21s and MiG–23/27s and comes complete with etched-brass leg restraints and firing-handles. Fulcrum and Flanker seats are promised for the future.

Also in PP Aeroparts range are a number of etched-brass Soviet aircraft ladders for the MiG–21, MiG–23 and, coming soon, the SU–27, plus a sheet of wheel chocks in different styles. Their sheet of etched-brass head-up displays can also be used – suitably modified – to represent Soviet versions. A dedicated set of Soviet HUDs is promised! Most of these etched-brass sheets of Soviet subjects also include on them a number of very delicate etchings of Odd-Rods IFF and Swift-Rods ILS aerials, angle-of-attack sensors, rear-view mirrors and temperature and pressure probes. All of these items will considerably enhance the appearance of any model to which they are applied.

For those who like their models in a diorama setting, PP also have a set of white-metal Warsaw Pact groundcrew and pilot in various poses, and Form-U-Lay has produced a printed sheet of Soviet hardstanding in the form of hexagonal paving slabs.

Finally, Scale Cast do a number of polyester resin conversion sets to convert single-seat kits into two-seaters. Those released so far cover the MiG–29 UB, SU–27 UB, SU–25UT and Yak–38U. Red Bear, another resin manufacturer, have a number of conversions in their range, including recce and two-seat versions of the MiG-25, two-seat SU-7 and YAK-38 and new noses for the Hasegawa MiG-23 and MiG-27.

5 MiG–15 FAGOT

TYPE: **SINGLE-SEAT FIGHTER**

ARMAMENT: **1 × 37mm N–37 and 2 × 23mm NR–23 cannon**

The revelation of the MiG–15 in combat over Korea came as an unpleasant surprise to American pilots. This new Soviet fighter could out-climb, out-accelerate, out-turn and had a greater ceiling than the latest US type, the North American F–86 Sabre.

Powered by an unlicensed derivative of the Rolls-Royce Nene turbojet, which had been supplied to the Soviets by the British government as a goodwill gesture, the design of the MiG–15 owed much to German research into swept-wing aircraft. About 8,000 MiG–15s were produced by the Soviet Union, in addition to substantial numbers licence-produced by the Polish and Czech aircraft industries. A later version with the 37mm cannon removed was fitted with an airborne interception radar mounted in the upper intake lip, and was designated MiG–15P.

Model

The best kit of the MiG–15 in 1:72 scale is the third offering from the Czech manufacturer KOVOZAVOD PROSTEJOV (KP). Two versions are available – the single-seat MiG–15bis and the two-seat trainer MiG–15 UTI.

Sold in a stout cardboard box with a cover illustration of a North Korean aircraft banking away after downing an F–86 Sabre, the accompanying instruction sheet is printed in Czech, English and German and gives painting details for a Czech aerobatic machine, a North Korean and an OSTRAVIAN (Czech) fighter-bomber. The decal sheet includes markings for all three aircraft although, in order to save printing costs, the multi-coloured badge on the Ostravian Air Regiment machine is supplied as a white shield with instructions to the modeller to hand-paint the badge using the drawing provided!

The single-seat kit itself is moulded in light grey plastic and comprises 54 parts, plus a two-piece stand and canopy in clear plastic.

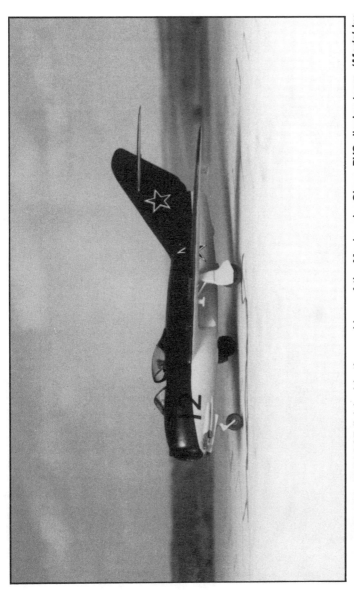

KP kit of the MiG–15 FAGOT finished in the markings of the Moskovsky Okrug PVO display team. (*Model by author; photo by Tim Perry*)

MiG–15 FAGOT. Note lack of wing markings on this machine. *(Model by author; photo by Tim Perry)*

The cockpit assembly consists of a bathtub with side consoles, an instrument panel, rudder pedals, control column and ejection seat. Colours are light grey with black instruments, control column and possibly dark green cushions on the seat.

The cockpit is cemented in place between the two vertically split fuselage halves, and the separate nosecone added. The fairing in the upper nose lip, which contains the gun-camera, should be drilled out to improve the appearance. Wings consist of upper and lower halves on each side, with cut-outs for the wheel-wells and feature commendably thin wing fences. Tailplane halves are supplied as single mouldings. The jetpipe is a separate moulding, as are the three undernose cannons. The appearance of these can be improved by replacing the barrels with suitable diameter Contrail tubing. The main undercarriage legs require the retraction jacks to be carefully bent into position as shown on the instructions, while the main doors need to be cut into three separate pieces using the moulded grooves as a guide. The nosegear is a single-piece moulding. Replace the rather cloudy canopy with an Aeroclub vacform item. Underwing stores consist of drop tanks, four rocket projectiles and two 10-round 'boxes' presumably containing folding-fin projectiles. In addition, two rocket-assisted take-off (RATO) pods are included for mounting under the rear fuselage.

Markings for a Soviet machine will have to be found in the spares box. I decided to finish mine in the colourful markings of the MOSKOVSKY OKRUG PVO aerobatic display team, with bright red upper surfaces and pale blue undersides and carrying no underwing stores. The finish is certainly different from all those 'silver' Soviet warplanes!

References

The Hamlyn Concise Guide to Soviet Military Aircraft
(HCG)   p74
The Observer's Soviet Directory
(*Observers*)   p160
Air International   Dec 1986
Air International   Jun 1985
(Colour side views)

6 MiG–17 FRESCO

TYPE: *SINGLE-SEAT FIGHTER*

ARMAMENT: *3 × 23mm NR–23 cannon (F & PF) plus 4 × AA–1 Alkali air-to-air missiles (PFU)*

The MiG–17 was a development of the MiG–15 with a longer rear fuselage to reduce drag and a new wing with greater sweepback and thinner section. Early models had the same engine as the MiG–15 but the main production version, the MiG–17F, was fitted with a simple afterburner. A limited all-weather interceptor version, the MiG–17PF, had radar fitted in a central inlet bullet and intake lip, while the MiG–17PFU introduced four AA–1 Alkali air-to-air missiles to become the Soviet Union's first missile-armed interceptor.

Although the MiG–17 was obsolescent by the mid-1960s, the FRESCO was much respected by the US pilots who encountered it in the skies over Vietnam.

Model

The only readily available kit of the MiG–17 is, fortunately, a reasonably accurate rendition of a MiG–17 PF produced by KP.

The model comes in a stout box with an excellent cover painting of a Czech-marked MiG–17PF, showing good detail. The instruction sheet is in English with profile drawings of the three options – Czech, Indonesian and Egyptian – available on the decal sheet.

Moulded in white plastic, the KP kit comprises 37 parts plus a two-part stand, combat-camera and canopy in clear plastic. Panel detail is in the form of rivets which, although fairly restrained, will still benefit from a light rub-down with fine wet-and-dry.

A full cockpit bathtub is provided with side consoles, an instrument panel with moulded-on radar scope, control column, rudder pedals and ejection seat.

The fuselage is in two halves with inserts for the nose intake and jetpipe. The nosecone may need a touch of filler to blend in. Wings are in upper and lower halves each side and have delicately moulded pitot tubes incorporated into the lower halves. These are

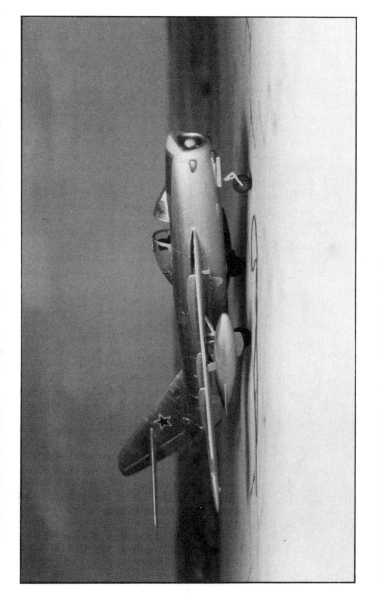

KP MiG–17PF FRESCO. *(Model by author; photo by Tim Perry)*

FRESCO kit finished with SNJ spray metal. Note black decal film for wing walkway with 'chipped' leading edge. *(Model by author; photo by Tim Perry)*

liable to breakage during construction and are best removed until later. The fin-mounted tailplanes are one-piece mouldings on either side. The main undercarriage legs are neat mouldings and require that their retraction jacks be gently bent forward before cementing in place. The doors need to be separated into three components each before being glued to the legs. The nosegear is a single moulding. Colours are medium grey for the legs and either grey or green for the wheel discs.

The Fresco-Ds 3-cannon armament is supplied as three varying lengths of rod which are best replaced by similar lengths of Contrail tubing for a more realistic appearance. Two drop tanks are supplied, as are the two wing-mounted radio-altimeter aerials and radio aerial. The canopy is a little on the brittle side and will benefit from cleaning up or replacing with an Aeroclub item. As no decals are included in the kit for a Soviet version, these will have to be obtained from other sources. Although I was able to find lots of photographs of foreign-marked 17PFs, the few shots of Soviet MiG–17s were of different versions.

Finish is bare metal overall, calling for the use of SNJ Spray Metal or Bare-Metal foil, this scheme being only relieved by the Soviet stars in six positions and the wing-root walkways in black, with lots of peeling, which is well shown on the box-art. The radomes are either off-white or green.

For those who wish to model other versions of the MiG–17, Aeroclub provide three vacform conversion kits specifically designed to go with the KP kit. These consist of vacform fuselages, and canopies with white-metal intake rings to create a Fresco-A or Fresco-C plus a replacement Fresco-D fuselage.

References

HCG	p75
Observers	p163
Air International	Jan 1987 p34
IPMS (UK) Magazine	Issue 1/1990

7 MiG-19 FARMER

TYPE: **SINGLE-SEAT FIGHTER**

ARMAMENT: *1 fuselage-mounted 37mm N-37 and*
2 × wing-root 23mm NR-23 cannon (MiG-19S)
or 4 × AA-1 Alkali AAMs (MiG-19PM)

The Soviet Union's first production supersonic fighter, the MiG-19 FARMER, was a logical development of the MiG-15 and MiG-17 designs, refined for supersonic performance. Powered by twin Mikulin AM-5 axial flow turbojets with a thrust of 4,850lbs each, the MiG-19 was a contemporary of the American F100 Super Sabre and the first flew in 1953, with deliveries of the production version, the MiG-19S, commencing in 1955. These had the Mikulins replaced with 5,732lb thrust Tumansky RD-9B engines. A limited all-weather capability was achieved with the introduction of the MiG-19PF, designated Farmer-B by NATO, which was fitted with ranging radar located in a central intake bullet and the upper lip of the intake. The final Soviet version, the MiG-19PM Farmer-D, retained the radar but replaced the cannon with 4 Alkali beam-riding air-to-air missiles on pylons, which projected ahead of the wing leading edge.

KP MiG-19 FARMER. (*Model by author; photo by Tim Perry*)

FARMER is airbrushed with SNJ spray metal. (*Model by author; photo by Tim Perry*)

Model

The best kit available in 1:72 scale is again from the Czech manufacturer KP. Although one of their earlier releases, it nevertheless makes up into a fine model of a cannon-armed MiG–19S.

Currently moulded in white plastic, the kit contains 69 parts, plus a two-part stand, gunsight, landing-light lens and canopy in clear plastic. No less than 25 of the parts comprise the various intakes, both large and small, which are dotted about the Farmer's airframe.

The instruction sheet is printed in Czech and includes drawings of the three versions – Czech, Soviet and Pakistani – depicted on the decal sheet.

The cockpit consists of an instrument panel, for which a decal is supplied, and a rather crude ejection seat, which is best replaced with an Aeroclub white-metal example. You will need to fashion a scratch-built floor and side consoles if the model is to be depicted with the canopy open.

The fuselage is in two halves, with the fin moulded integrally with the port half, and has very fine panel detail. Nosecone and jet efflux are separate parts with inserts for the afterburners, and the wings are in upper and lower halves on each side. The tailplanes are single-piece items port and starboard. The main cannon armament is rather lumpy and is best replaced with Contrail tubing to represent the cannon muzzles. As I mentioned earlier, the numerous intakes dotted about the fuselage are moulded as separate items which require careful removal from the sprue, cleaning up and attaching to the model. Their locations are marked on the fuselage by tiny vee shapes, which require constant cross-checking with the instructions to ensure correct placement. A number of spare intakes are included to cover 'losses'.

Mainwheels are moulded separately from the legs, while the nosewheel is a single moulding.

Two 2-part drop tanks are included, as are two UV–8–57 8-round 55mm rocket pods and their curious backward pointing pylons, designed to clear the maingear wells. No locating holes are supplied for the drop tanks or rocket pods, their positions being simply marked by engravings on the wing undersurface. The same comment also applies to the radio altimeter antennae, radio aerial and pitot head, so these items are best attached using super-glue to ensure a strong join. The canopy is in KP's usual, rather brittle, clear plastic, so take care if you clean it up. Aeroclub supply a vacform replacement. Finish is plain metal with red stars in the usual six positions and a two-digit aircraft number on either side of the nose.

Conversion possibilities are limited, although the MiG–19PM could be a fairly easy option, requiring the addition of the radar in the nose and four scratch-built Alkali missiles.

References

HCG	p80
Observers	p166
Air International	Feb 1987
Takeoff	Numbers 100 & 101

8 MiG-21 FISHBED

TYPE: **SINGLE-SEAT INTERCEPTOR**

ARMAMENT: **1 × twin-barrelled GSh-23 gunpack (MiG-21bis) plus 2 × AA-2 Atoll and 2 × AA-8 Aphids**

Perhaps the most famous of all Soviet fighters, the MiG-21, dubbed FISHBED by NATO, owes its origins to the Korean war. A contemporary of the Lockheed F-104 Starfighter, the MiG-21 was designed as a simple day-only interceptor, powered by the then new Tumanksy R11 turbojet and armed with a single 30mm cannon and two AA-2 Atoll IR AAMs. It entered service with the Soviet Air Force in 1959. The MiG-21 has undergone such a host of changes during its lifetime – with uprated engines, revised and enlarged vertical fin, improved radar and armament, different canopy shapes and increasingly larger dorsal spines in each variant – that the final production version, Fishbed-N in NATO parlance, bears only a passing resemblance to the initial Fishbed-C.

Probably one of the most produced and exported jet fighters in the world, the MiG-21 is being replaced in Soviet service by the much more potent MiG-29 Fulcrum, but the type is still in service with a number of air forces and has been developed into later versions by the Chinese as the XIAN J-7 and J-8 series.

Model

With so many different versions of the MiG-21, the modeller could make a large collection of models on just this one type alone. Unfortunately, all the versions are not covered by the available kits of the type; indeed the only accurate kit, from KP, represents a later type MiG-21MF Fishbed-J. Matchbox have kitted a MiG-21 which, in its original guise, represented a MiG-21PF Fishbed-D. This has been re-released as a MiG-21MF Fishbed-J but it is inaccurate for either version. The early generation MiG-21F has been attempted by both Hasegawa and Airfix but, again, neither version accurately portrays the real thing – both models are decidedly out-of-scale.

KP MiG–21 FISHBED. Note PP Aeroparts ladder. (Model by author; photo by Tim Perry)

All is not lost, however, as Fujimi are about to release a range of kits of the MiG–21 which, if their F–4 Phantom kits are anything to go by, will at last provide accurate models of the whole Fishbed family. Releases announced are the MiG–21bis, SMT, MF, RF, F, U, PF EARLY AND LATE.

Until that happy event, the modeller is left with the KP kit which is, at least, a reasonable attempt at a Fishbed-J.

Consisting of 58 parts moulded in white plastic with very restrained raised panel detail, plus a clear canopy and two landing-lights, KP's kit represents a MiG-21 MF. The accompanying instruction sheet is printed in Czech, English and German and provides three-view drawings for the four options covered by the decal sheet, namely two camouflaged plus a silver Czech machine and an all-silver Hungarian example. Also included on the sheet are five decals for the cockpit consisting of side panels, consoles and an instrument panel plus a decal representing the seat straps.

Construction starts with the cockpit which consists of a floor with side consoles, a rear bulkhead and seat plus an instrument panel and rudder pedals.

The nosecone is moulded as a separate insert, as is the rear face of the engine. With these and the cockpit assembly cemented in place, the two fuselage halves are cemented together. The complete fin and rudder is moulded with the starboard fuselage half, which leaves a prominent gap in the port half where the spine meets the fin, which will need the application of filler to hide it. The various engine bay cooling intakes are supplied as separate mouldings, which will benefit from cleaning up with a sharp knife and having holes drilled into their front faces. A separate intake ring completes the fuselage assembly.

The wings and tailplanes are single-piece mouldings port and starboard and require only the attention of the craft knife to remove the small amount of flash before being cemented to the fuselage.

The undercarriage consists of rather crudely moulded main legs with separate retraction jacks. The locating holes in the wings are very shallow, necessitating the use of super-glue to affix the legs in place. The precise location of the jacks is not clear from the moulding, so a close study of the assembly drawings is required to create a strong enough undercarriage. The main leg doors require their lower portions to be canted outwards, and this is achieved by carefully bending the door along the moulded crease. The main doors have interior detail moulded onto their inner faces, as have the fuselage wells.

The nosewheel and leg are moulded as a single piece, while the

SNJ spray-metal-finished MiG–21. (*Model by author; photo by Tim Perry*)

mainwheels, with neatly moulded brake drums, are separate items.

Deflectors for the blow-in doors, pitot head, Odd-Rods IFF aerials, nose-probe and wing-mounted radio altimeter aerials are all moulded individually, but their attachment requires great care as there are no locating holes, merely raised marks indicating their position.

Armament options consist of an underfuselage GSh–23 twin-barrelled gunpack which requires the addition of barrels from sprue plus two AA–2 Atoll Sidewinder copies and two rocket launchers.

I must mention here the super detail set from PP Aeroparts. This consists of etched-brass parts to enhance the plastic kit. The parts were designed with the Fujimi MiG–21 in mind but are equally applicable to the KP kit. Cockpit detail comes in the form of an instrument panel with etched detail.

A white-metal ejection seat is supplied, together with etched-brass leg restraints and firing handles. An afterburner ring and highly detailed variable jet nozzle are included, as is interior detailing for all three fuselage air brakes. Mainwheel hubs and brake discs, u/c doors, scissor-links for the main legs and all the fences are provided. The sheet also includes a host of aerials and sensors, ILS, IFF, AOA, pitch and yaw vanes, etc.

References

Scale Models International	May 1989
Scale Models International	Nov 1989
Scale Models International	Dec 1989
Takeoff	numbers 41, 42 & 43

IPMS Finland publications
MiG–21 Fishbed in Color – Squadron/Signal

9 MiG-23 FLOGGER-B

TYPE: **SINGLE-SEAT MULTI-ROLE FIGHTER**

ARMAMENT: *1 internal 23mm GSh twin-barrel cannon plus two wing-glove pylons for AA–7 Apex and two belly pylons for AA–8 Aphids*

The NATO reporting name FLOGGER actually refers to a whole family of aircraft which have been developed from the prototype MiG–23 which first appeared at the Domodedovo air display in July 1967 and was designated Flogger-A by the ASCC.

Representing the Soviet Union's first successful application of variable-geometry, the Flogger is powered by a single Tumanksy R–29B afterburning turbofan of some 25,000lbs thrust. Fitted with High-Lark radar, said to be comparable to that in the McDonnell-Douglas F–4 Phantom, the Flogger features an unusual, though neat and robust, wide-track undercarriage which folds into the fuselage, a retractable ventral fin, twin nosewheels with mud-guards and a massive vertical fin.

A number of variants have been produced apart from the initial service version, the Flogger-B. Flogger-C is a tandem two-seat trainer, Flogger-D is a dedicated ground-attack variant (see MiG–27), Flogger-E is an export version of B with less capable radar and avionics fit, and Flogger-F is a hybrid combining the Flogger-D's airframe with the B's engine, variable intakes and internal cannon. Flogger-G introduced a smaller fin with the leading-edge fillet removed and is fitted with a more advanced radar as well as larger nosewheels with bulged doors and an undernose sensor pod. Flogger-H is an export version of F, J is an improved D, while Flogger-K is the latest development of the Flogger-G with dog-tooth notches on the wing gloves, improved avionics, smaller wing glove and swivelling wing pylons. Reportedly, it can carry the newer improved AA–11 Archer AAMs.

Model

Two 1:72 scale kits are currently available – from Airfix and Hasegawa – both depicting the earlier MiG–23M Flogger-B.

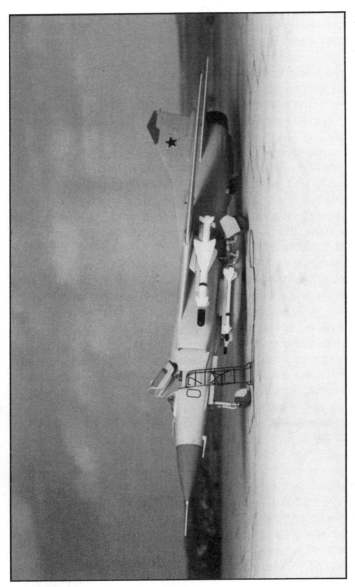

Hasegawa MiG–23 FLOGGER-B with PP ladder. Finish is air superiority grey. *(Model by author; photo by Tim Perry)*

Although both kits are basically accurate, Hasegawa's is much more delicate and has the usual crisp appearance associated with that manufacturer.

Containing some 50 parts moulded in light grey plastic and a four-part clear sprue with two landing-lights, a windscreen and separate canopy, Hasegawa's kit has the usual style of fine raised panel detail.

A combined cockpit floor and nosewheel bay is supplied, together with an instrument panel for which a decal is included on the sheet. The control column is moulded with the nose under-carriage leg and protrudes through a hole in the wheel-well when the nosegear is added at a later stage.

The armchair-style ejection seat should be replaced with an Aeroclub white-metal item. As with most swing-wing models, the fuselage is split horizontally at the rear with the forward portion being split vertically, the joint being partially hidden by the intakes.

The model's appearance can be improved by inserting a 3mm plug between the fuselage and the separate nosecone before you cement the latter item in place.

The wings are single-piece mouldings, port and starboard with a dog-tooth arrangement to allow them to pivot together. The vertical fin is a single item, while the intakes feature separately moulded splitter plates and landing-light lenses. Single-part tailplanes, a two-part ventral fin which allows both folded and extended configurations and an afterburner nozzle complete the major airframe assembly. The complex maingear legs are in two separate parts, which results in a very delicate appearance but a rather weak assembly. I recommend the use of super-glue to ensure a strong joint.

The mainwheels arc neal mouldings while the doors feature internal detail, but the two doors which act as mudguards are attached to the wheels themselves rather than the legs which, I am sure, is not the arrangement on the real thing! The twin nosewheels with integrally moulded mudguards are attached to the single-part noseleg and the nose doors need to be carefully separated along the moulded joint line.

Three delicately moulded pitots are included – one for the nose tip and two fuselage-mounted. The Odd-Rods antenna should be replaced by PP Aeroparts items. Armament supplied in the kit consists of a ventral gunpack plus two AA–7 Apex and two AA–8 Aphids and their associated pylons. These examples are inaccu-rate – particularly the Apex's – and should be replaced with scratch-built items.

Note 'outstanding unit' symbol on nose. (*Model by author; photo by Tim Perry*)

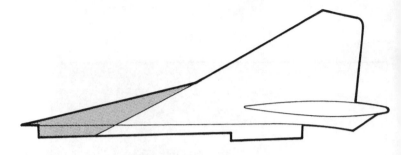

Fig. 1 Remove shaded section

The crystal-clear canopy features a 'lug' on its rear end which allows it to fit into a slot in the fuselage either in the closed or open position – a very neat arrangement.

The painting guide and decal sheet give details of a camouflaged machine with Gunze Sangyo colours being quoted. A simple alternative is an overall air-superiority grey scheme or all-silver, which was the finish depicted when the kit was first released.

A more drastic alteration to the kit is to convert it into the later Flogger-G variant. The major modification involves a reduction in fin area by the removal of the dorsal fillet. This is achieved by sawing away the leading edge from the existing kink to a point 23mm from its front end (see Fig. 1). The flat section left behind is restored to an aerodynamic shape by careful sanding, and the resultant slot in the upper fuselage is filled with plastic card smoothed in with filler.

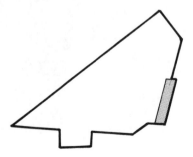

Fig. 2 Add shaded section

The horizontal tailplanes have a kinked trailing edge which is modelled by the addition of a sliver of plastic card 6mm in length cemented to the trailing edge and blended in by careful sanding (see Fig. 2).

The large undernose IR sensor must be removed and the jetpipe shortened by 3mm at its rear face. A suitable drop tank from the spares box can be added to a scratch-built central pylon. Later Soviet Floggers sport a three-colour upper surface camouflage scheme with pale blue undersides. The upper surface colours appear to be dark green, stone and tan which are closely matched by DBI Forest Green (CAC2), Light Stone (CBC22) and Tan (CAC6) while the undersurface blue is DBI Pale Blue (CAC21).

References

HCG	p100
Air International	Dec 1978
Air International	Jan 1987
Warplane	No 78
Scale Models International	Jan 1980
Scale Models International	Feb 1989

MiG–23/27 Flogger – Osprey
Combat Aircraft Series
IPMS Finland Special Publication
MiG–23/27 Flogger in Action
   (Squadron/Signal Publications)

10 MiG–25 FOXBAT

TYPE: *SINGLE-SEAT INTERCEPTOR*

ARMAMENT: *4 × AA–6 Acrid AAMs (2 SARH & 2 IR)*

The MiG–25 FOXBAT probably epitomises, more than most aircraft, the East-West arms race. When it looked as though SAC's B–52s would have increasing difficulty in penetrating Soviet air defences, the Americans began to develop the Mach–3, 70,000ft ceiling, XB–70 Valkyrie strategic bomber. Consequently, the Russians developed the Foxbat to counter this threat. The XB–70 was cancelled but the threat then posed by the MiG–25 led to the development of the McDonnell-Douglas F–15 Eagle interceptor by the US and its subsequent sale to the Israelis to enable the Chel Ha'avir to catch overflying Syrian MiG–25s.

First flown around 1964, the Foxbat is a large twin-finned interceptor powered by two 27,000lb thrust Tumansky R–31 afterburning turbojets fed by massive wedge-shaped intakes. The huge nose-radar is believed to be a development of the TU–28P set and is coded Fox-Fire by NATO. Similarly its armament, the

Hasegawa MiG–25 FOXBAT with PP Warpac white-metal figures. (*Model by author; photo by Tim Perry*)

MiG–25 FOXBAT. (*Model by author; photo by Tim Perry*)

AA–6 Acrid, by far the world's largest air-to-air missile, owes much to the TU–28P's AA–5 ASH.

Details of the Foxbat were revealed to the West when a Soviet MiG–25, piloted by the defecting Lt Belenko, landed at Hakodate airport in Japan. The aircraft was returned to the Soviet Union, but not before Japanese and US intelligence experts had pored over it. Essentially a straight-line bomber interceptor rather than a dog-fighter, the MiG–25 has been developed into the reconnaissance MiG–25R, the ELINT MiG–25D and the two-seat trainer, the MiG–25U. Early reports of a two-seat 'Super MiG–25' with improved radar and armament were confirmed by the appearance of the MiG–31 Foxhound.

Model

The only 1:72 scale kit of a MiG–25 is that from the Japanese firm of Hasegawa. Fortunately it is accurate – Hasegawa were prob-ably at Hakodate airport before the intelligence teams!

Moulded in Hasegawa's usual style of light grey plastic, the kit consists of 53 parts with fine-line raised panel detail plus a beautifully clear canopy. Cockpit assembly consists of a simple bathtub which is cemented onto a detailed nosewheel bay. A decal is included for the instrument panel while the seat, the usual armchair, should be replaced with an Aeroclub white-metal item. A control column made from stretched sprue will need to be added to the otherwise bare cockpit.

The fuselage is in two vertically split halves with inserts for top and bottom rear fuselage. These inserts are probably necessary to achieve the correct cross-section in the mould, but they do require slight amounts of filler to hide the join lines. The fuselage halves have moulded-on aerials and Odd-Rods IFF antenna which, although very delicate, do get in the way when rubbing down to eliminate the joint lines. It is better to remove these items carefully and re-cement them in place after painting. The Odd-Rods aerials can be replaced with PP Aeroparts etched-brass items.

A rear end with inter-nozzle fairing is added to the fuselage, as are the two massive exhaust nozzles which are rather shallow, although this can be hidden by fitting circular blanking plates, painted red, to each nozzle. Horizontal tails and ventral fins are separate items, moulded as single pieces. The wings are in two pieces either side, with a large upper half incorporating the wingtip fairing and a smaller lower insert – this form of construction results in a commendably thin trailing edge. The huge intakes comprise outer sections, to which are added the inner splitter plates, before the whole assembly is cemented to the fuselage.

The undercarriage consists of massive mainwheels moulded in two halves which are attached to simple one-piece legs and a twin-wheel nosegear – again with a single-piece leg. The maingear doors are provided as single pieces, with a moulded-in groove allowing them to be cut and separated into two doors on either side if the gear is in the extended position. Similarly, the nose door has to be separated into no less than five pieces, before being cemented into place.

The only other additions needed to complete the model are the nose-probe, side-mounted pitot tube and armament, which comprises two Semi-Active Radar Homing and two Infra-Red AA–6 Acrid missiles, each of which is made up from three parts plus their associated pylons.

The instruction sheet shows colours schemes and markings for two aircraft, Lt Belenko's number 31 and an unknown example coded 07. Both schemes are in light grey, although the paint mix numbers quoted are probably Gunze Sangyo or some other Japanese manufacturer. Any suitable light grey will probably suffice as will dark grey for the nosecone and dielectric panels.

Jet nozzles can be painted with Humbrol's Polished Steel, while the fuselage rear end is a mixture of silver and brown to represent the exhaust staining in this area. Missiles are black and white with red control surfaces.

References

HGC   p108
Red Star Rising Doug Richardson (Hamlyn)
Warplane   No 79

11 MiG–27 FLOGGER-D

TYPE: *SINGLE-SEAT GROUND-ATTACK FIGHTER*

ARMAMENT: *1 × six-barrel rotary cannon and hardpoints under the intake ducts, rear fuselage, and wing gloves plus fixed pylons under the wings capable of carrying a maximum load of approx 6,600lbs*

Derived from the MiG–23, the MiG–27 retains the same NATO reporting name of FLOGGER, although with the suffix letters D and J. This aircraft is the dedicated ground-attack variant of the same basic design. The most obvious external feature is the redesigned 'duck-bill' nose to give the pilot an improved view of the ground ahead of and below the aircraft. A small ranging radar is fitted at its tip, aft of which is a laser ranging device and a Doppler aerial. The pilot is protected from ground fire by additional armour added to the cockpit sides, and the intakes are of simplified design, lacking the splitter plates of the MiG–23, while the variable-nozzle jetpipe has given way to a lighter fixed design. Also fitted are larger low-pressure mainwheel tyres with bulged undercarriage doors.

An updated version, Flogger-J, was identified in 1981 and has

Hasegawa MiG–27 FLOGGER-D. (*Model by author; photo by Tim Perry*)

FLOGGER-D. (*Model by author; photo by Tim Perry*)

various changes to the avionics fit and wing root leading-edge extensions, possibly housing ECM equipment.

Model

The only 1:72 kit of the Flogger-D released so far is that from Hasegawa which is obviously based on their MiG–23 kit with detail differences as appropriate. It even features exactly the same construction drawings, complete with a MiG–23 nose and variable nozzle, although the revised intakes are redrawn, as is the armament fit. Fortunately, a new nose is supplied as well as the revised nozzle, intakes and a recontoured windscreen.

Construction follows the same sequence as the MiG–23, apart from the revised stores, which consist of the six-barrelled cannon, two AA–2 Atoll AAMs, two rocket pods, two bombs and two drop tanks plus their associated pylons. Note that the wing pylons are fixed, do not swivel with the wings and are only fitted for ferry purposes.

When first released, Hasegawa's Floggers featured an instruction sheet in English which named all the parts, such as the ILS antenna, AA–2 missiles etc. It had a potted history of the type and gave a choice of two paint finishes, all-silver and camouflaged, all included on the decal sheet. Since being re-released, the box-art has improved but the instruction sheet is now multi-lingual with all the parts merely being numbered. The decal sheet, although more comprehensive, with stencil data, etc, gives only a single choice of a camouflaged machine for which Gunze Sangyo numbers are quoted and even the potted history is reduced to a few lines.

References
HCG	p118
Warplane	No 79
Air International	Jan 1987
Scale Models International	Feb 1989

MiG–23/27 Flogger – Osprey
Combat Aircraft Series
MiG–23/27 Flogger in Action
   (Squadron/Signal Publications)

12   MiG–29 FULCRUM

TYPE: SINGLE-SEAT AIR-SUPERIORITY FIGHTER

ARMAMENT: 1 internal 30mm cannon, 2 × AA–10 Alamo long-range SARH AAMs and 4 × AA–8 Aphid IR AAMs plus a centre fuselage pylon for droptank

If ever a single aircraft laid to rest the myth of Soviet inferiority in aircraft design it was the MiG–29 FULCRUM. Revealed by US reconnaissance satellites at the Ramenskoye flight test center in 1978 and designated RAM-L by US Intelligence, the MiG–29 was shown to the West for the first time in 1986 when six aircraft made a goodwill visit to Finland. Its first public appearance in the West was at the 1988 Farnborough show, where its performance and flying display dazzled both public and participating pilots. Not only were its flight characteristics demonstrated, but also the two Mikoyan test pilots and the Fulcrum's designers were there to answer questions about the new fighter.

Powered by a pair of Tumanksy RD–33 afterburning turbofans with a thrust of 18,300lbs, the MiG–29 features a unique engine intake arrangement to prevent foreign object damage from debris thrown up by the nosewheel during take-off and landing. The intakes have ramps which close off the front of the inlets, air being fed to the engines via louvres above the wing roots. Some Western experts were surprised by the MiG's lack of a fly-by-wire control system although, from its flight performance, such an omission does not seem to affect its agility. The aircraft is fitted with an advanced pulse Doppler radar and an infra-red search and track system mounted in a glass dome just forward of the windscreen. For its Farnborough appearance, the aircraft carried no external armament but the aircraft has been photographed carrying two AA–10 Alamo long-range radar guided AAMs on the inner wing pylons and four AA–8 Aphid short-range infra-red guided AAMs on the outer wing pylons, so presumably this is a standard fit.

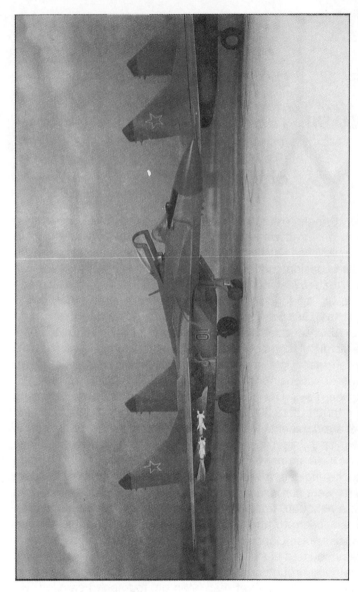

Hasegawa MiG-29 FULCRUM with scratchbuilt AA-8 Aphids, covers over upper intakes and 'Remove Before Flight' tags. (*Model by author; photo by Tim Perry*)

Model

Hasegawa was the first to release a kit of the Fulcrum using data obtained from the types' appearance in Finland in 1986. Unfortunately, the dimensions are inaccurate, being too short in length and too great in span. The kit is well moulded in Hasegawa's usual crisp style and certainly captures the look of the original. The kit was re-released following the aircraft's Farnborough appearance, but the hoped-for retooling was confined to the revision of the rudder chord. A sprue containing weapons was also included.

The second attempt at a Fulcrum was an offering from Fujimi which, following their highly successful Phantom family, was expected to be a good rendition. Again the results were disappointing and the kit is still dimensionally incorrect, with the added error of a cockpit canopy that is too flat and wide.

The third release was by ESCI, which is almost a copy of the Fujimi kit and is still not the right size. Italeri, Airfix and Heller have all announced the release, during 1990, of kits of the Fulcrum, both single- and two-seat versions. Until they appear, the most accurate release to date is that from Revell of a single-seat MiG–29A Fulcrum, which has been followed recently by a kit of the two-seat MiG–29UB. Numerous scale plans have been published in various magazines, notably in *Fine Scale Modeller* of July 1989, *Airfix Magazine* of February 1989 and *Air Forces International* of December 1988, and all vary in size and shape. All I can say is that, based on the manufacturer's published dimensions of a length *including probe* of 17.32m and a span of 11.36m, the equivalent sizes in 1:72 scale are, according to my calculator, 240.5mm and 157.7mm respectively. Revell's kit checks in at 237mm and 170mm so the wingspan needs to be reduced by some 12mm to be strictly accurate.

The model comes in a stout cardboard box with a nondescript cover painting of a Fulcrum being chased by an F–16. The kit is neatly moulded in light grey plastic with very fine engraved panel detail and consists of 71 parts plus a clear sprue containing a windscreen, canopy and IR ball. A cockpit bathtub with side consoles for which decals are supplied, a control column, instrument panel with decal and ejection seat make up the 'office', although the ejection seat resembles a large comfy armchair and is best replaced with an Aeroclub or PP Aeroparts white-metal item. The fuselage is split horizontally and two pieces are provided to represent the engine compressor faces. Before cementing the fuselage halves together, I would recommend that you drill out the cannon trough and fit a muzzle from the inside using a short length

Hasegawa FULCRUM. *(Model by author; photo by Tim Perry)*

of Contrail tube. One major inaccuracy in Revell's kit concerns the fuselage spine which should end just in front of the air brake, between the jetpipes. Revell have moulded this so that it extends all the way to the tail, although their three-view drawing clearly shows the correct layout, as well as showing the cooling intake on the rear port side of the spine, which is not even included in the kit. To remedy this defect, fill the rear end of the spine with Milliput and, when it's dry, carefully pare away the plastic to shorten the spine. You will probably go all the way through the plastic, which is where the Milliput comes in.

Make good the surface by filling and gentle sanding, and add the intake made from scrap plastic before cementing both fuselage halves together. The intakes are in two halves either side with a separate FOD blanking plate, which is shown on the instruction sheet as being cemented in the closed position, whereas most head-on photographs of parked Fulcrums show the doors to be retracted, i.e. open.

The jetpipes do not have the distinctive concentric double-walled appearance of the real thing, so they can either be replaced by Hasegawa items or blanked off to hide the orifice. The wings, tailplanes and vertical fins are all single-piece mouldings, and the only alteration necessary is the reduction in wingspan by removing 6mm from each tip and carving back to the original shape. The wingtip housings with a navigation light at the front end and spherical radar warning ball at the rear can be added from scrap sprue. The aircraft displayed at Farnborough and Paris had extended chord rudders, so these will need to be depicted by carefully removing the kit rudders and adding new ones made from thin plastic card, sanded to airfoil section. The nosewheel and leg are delicate mouldings although the leg is in separate upper and lower sections, which results in a weak join unless super-glue is used to attach the two parts. Strictly speaking, the retraction jack and its door on the front of the leg should be offset to starboard which will entail the cutting of a new slot in the wheel bay, blanking off the old slot, removal of the jack and repositioning it on the starboard side of the leg.

The nosewheels on the Fulcrum are fitted with a small mesh mudguard which is not included in any of the kits released so far. For accuracy's sake, one should be added from scrap plastic, although its shape is rather complex. A simpler alternative is to ignore it completely, as the Fulcrums which visited Finland did not have this item fitted, nor can it be seen on the example photographed in the Soviet Union by USAF observers in 1988. Main-

Revell MiG FULCRUM with PP ladder and chocks. (*Model by John Mock; photo by Tim Perry*)

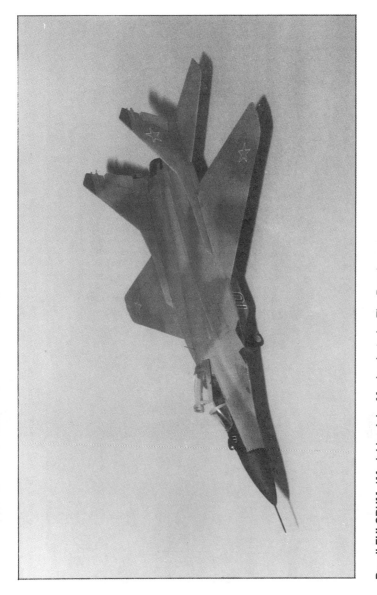

Revell FULCRUM. *(Model by John Mock; photo by Tim Perry)*

Side-by-side view of Hasegawa's undersized and Revell's more accurate version with corrected wingspan. *(Photo by Tim Perry)*

wheels can be used straight from the kit but the main doors require the addition of a landing-light, made from scrap plastic, cemented to the forward edge. The canopy can be cemented in the open or closed positions and the various pitots and aerials added.

The MiG–29 cries out for the addition of ILS antennae, Odd-Rods IFF aerials, angle-of-attack sensors, rear-view mirrors etc., all of which are to be found in the PP Aeroparts etched-brass range. Revell's armament consists of six nondescript missiles, which appear to be propeller-driven as their rear fins are angled at 45 degrees to the longitudinal! Also included are four AA–8 Aphids which are rather more accurate. Any modellers requiring AA–10 Alamos will have to scratch-build their own or obtain samples from Hasegawa's kit.

Four-view drawings for three aircraft are included on the instruction sheet, which quotes Revell paint numbers and gives mixing instructions to achieve the correct shades where necessary. The very comprehensive decal sheet contains stencil data and all the dark grey dielectric panels, as well as markings for an Indian, GDR or Soviet machine. The GDR and Soviet markings include two sets of numerals 0–9 enabling any machine to be modelled.

References

MiG–29 Soviet Superfighter Jon Lake (Osprey)
Red Star Rising Doug Richardson (Hamlyn)

Air International	Dec 1988
Air Forces Monthly	Dec 1988
Warplane	No 78
Take-off	No 35
Fine Scale Modeler	Jul 1989

13 MiG–31 FOXHOUND

TYPE: *TWO-SEAT ALL-WEATHER INTERCEPTOR*

ARMAMENT: *4 × AA–9 Amos long-range radar guided*
AAMs on fuselage pylons plus 4 × AA–8 Aphid
short-range infra-red AAMs

Evidence that the MiG OKB were developing a 'Super-Foxbat' was revealed to the West by the defecting MiG–25 pilot Lt Belenko, who told US intelligence officials of a two-seat development of the Foxbat. Clearly owing much to the earlier aircraft, the FOXHOUND incorporates updated avionics and aerodynamic improvements. As well as the two-man cockpit, the MiG–31 differs from its predecessor in having small leading-edge root extensions (LERXs), a longer fuselage, longer jetpipes, simpler engine inlets, a new pulse-Doppler radar allowing full look-down/shoot-down capability and track-while-scan operating modes. Also new is the Foxhound's primary armament – four AA–9 Amos long-range missiles mounted in tandem pairs under the fuselage, similar to the Hughes AIM–54 Phoenix of the F–14 Tomcat, plus four AA–8 Aphids mounted in pairs on each inner wing pylon.

Another major difference between the Foxbat and the Foxhound concerns the main landing gear. Most published drawings of the MiG–31 depict a twin side-by-side arrangement similar to that of the Sepecat jaguar which, in *Jane's All the World's Aircraft*, is described as being steerable to cater for cross-wind landings. However, in an article published in *Aviation Week and Space Technology* of 5 June 1989, a visiting US delegation report an interview with MiG OKB designer Rostislav Belyakov, in which he states 'the MiG–31 has a modified main landing gear to improve operations from soft fields. The maingear has two wheels in tandem, with the trailing wheel offset so that its track is outside that of the forward wheel'. *Jane's* have amended their drawing in the latest edition.

Model

The only 1:72 scale model of the MiG–31 so far released is that

Revell MiG–31 FOXHOUND. Oversize mainwheels have been replaced from the spares box. *(Model by John Mock; photo by Tim Perry)*

kitted by Revell, which appears to be an accurate rendition and which, fortunately, incorporates the tandem twin-wheel maingear mentioned previously.

Comprising 99 parts moulded in light grey plastic with etched panel detail plus a clear sprue containing a two-part cockpit canopy, Revell's Foxhound comes in a stout cardboard box with very off-putting box-art which does not do justice to the contents. A cockpit floor with side consoles is included, onto which are mounted the two 3-part ejection seats and two control columns. Decals are supplied for the consoles and instrument panel, although the whole arrangement must be purely speculative since little can be seen with the canopies in the closed position. I prefer to cut through the canopies of my models and cement them in the open position to show the interior detail but I have yet to see a photograph of a Foxhound with the canopy open, although I imagine it is a twin clamshell arrangement. Until proof is forth-coming, they will remain firmly closed!

The forward fuselage is in two vertically split halves with a separate nosecone, while the main fuselage consists of upper and lower halves with an end-piece and twin jetpipes. With the forward fuselage cemented to the rear, the huge intakes are added. These consist of an inner splitter plate and a three-sided box on either side. Revell have moulded a curious shutter arrangement, looking like a washboard, which is supposed to be cemented into the intake. Again, this is pure speculation, so I left these items off my model.

The large wings are in two parts either side – a top surface and an insert for the underside – while the fins and tailplanes are moulded as single pieces. Detail parts comprise the suction-relief doors on the top and bottom of the intakes, plus a variety of lumps and bumps, including the intake-mounted ECM fairings. These appear to be undersized, so they are best replaced with suitably-shaped scrap plastic.

Each main undercarriage consists of a large leg with the trailing beam axle, plus a separate vee-strut arrangement, to which are cemented the two large 2-part mainwheels. Two-part doors, which would benefit from being thinned down, complete the maingear. While the arrangement appears to be correct, the detail must be suspect, particularly in the size of the mainwheels, the track and the shape of the doors. The only photograph I have seen so far of a Foxhound on the ground is a three-quarter front view of a taxying example, which shows a maingear sloping out from the bay, with what might be an offset tandem arrangement. What

Revell FOXHOUND. (Model by John Mock; photo by Tim Perry)

Side-by-side view of MiG–25 FOXBAT and 'SUPER FOXBAT', MiG–31 FOXHOUND. Note revised cockpit, nose, wings, jetpipes and undercarriage on latter. (*Photo by Tim Perry*)

is clear is that the wheels are smaller than Revell's, are closer together and that the doors consist of a top-hinged side door plus a forward-hinged longitudinal door, which appears also to act as an air brake.

However, until more data appears, we are stuck with Revell's offering. The nosewheel, thankfully, is accurate and complete with a rather thick mudguard. Included in Revell's kit are two large underwing tanks with deeply etched panel lines, which are best filled if the tanks are used. Four 2-part representations of the Foxhound's primary armament, the AA–9 Amos missiles, are also included, which look reasonably accurate according to published data currently available. They would benefit from having their conical nosecones sanded to a more rounded shape.

The other two missiles in the kit are, I think, meant to be AA–6 Acrids, which Revell's plan-view shows as being mounted on the inner wing pylons with the drop tanks on the outer pylons, although the construction drawing shows the reverse, with the tanks on the inner pylons! Both drawings have the four AA–9s mounted in tandem pairs under the fuselage.

A more representative arrangement, confirmed from photographs, is four underfuselage AA–9s plus four AA–8 Aphids on a twin mounting on the inner pylon and no drop tanks. The AA–8s can be scratch-built or obtained from Esci's Kamov KA–34 Hokum kit. Revell's excellent decal sheet contains a host of stencil data, all the dark grey dielectric panels, an anti-glare panel in black, instrument panel and consoles, six red stars and numerals 0–9. The three-view drawing shows a simple paint scheme of overall blue-grey with light grey undersides, although published colour photographs of Foxhound seem to indicate an overall medium grey colour.

References
Red Star Rising Doug Richardson (Hamlyn)

14 SUKHOI SU–7 FITTER A

TYPE: *SINGLE-SEAT FIGHTER-BOMBER*

ARMAMENT: *2 × 30mm NR–30 cannon plus four underwing and two fuselage pylons capable of carrying approx. 2,200lbs of ordnance when ventral drop tanks are carried*

First revealed to the West at the Tushino Aviation Day in Moscow on 24 June 1956, the S–1, as the prototype was designated, was viewed by Western aviation experts as a smaller and lighter contemporary of the Republic F–105 Thunderchief. Possessing a highly-swept (62 degrees at the leading edge), relatively thick wing, the SU–7 offered supersonic speed combined with low gust-response giving a stable ride at low level, although such a configuration was to result in a rather mediocre airfield performance.

The Sukhoi SU–7, which was given the code-name FITTER by the ASCC, is armed with two wing-root 30mm Nudelmann-Richter cannons with a modest 70 RPG. Six stores pylons are fitted – two under the fuselage and two on each wing, one outboard of the wheel-well and another beyond the large wing fence. To supplement the modest internal fuel capacity, the two under-fuselage pylons are almost always occupied by two 132 imp. gal. drop tanks.

Power is provided by a massive Lyulka AL–7F turbojet, estimated to have a thrust rating of 14,200lbs dry and 22,046lbs with reheat.

A brute of a fighter, the SU–7, in its Fitter-A version, is now approaching obsolescence and has been replaced in Soviet service by its swing-wing derivative, the Sukhoi SU–17/20/22 Fitter-C to K, although the type is still in Czech and Polish service.

Model
The best injection-moulded kit in 1:72 scale is that from KP which depicts the SU–7 BKL Fitter-A version, equipped with a larger nosewheel, requiring a bulged door and unusual mainwheel-

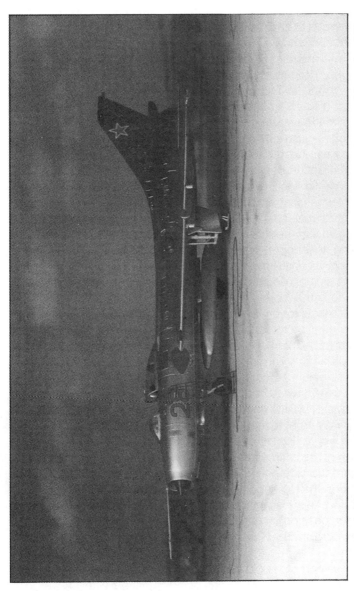

KP Sukhoi SU-7 BKL FITTER-B with PP ladder. Note 'KL' skids on maingear, gun blast panel from decal film and exhaust louvres on fuselage above mainwheel. (*Model by author; photo by Tim Perry*)

mounted skids to enhance performance when operating from short, semi-prepared airstrips. These skids, (KOLO LIZHNI – from which the aircraft gets its KL designation), are hydraulically activated, and can be retracted for operation from paved runways or extended to bear part of the aircraft's weight when soft surfaces are encountered.

KP's kit contains 82 parts moulded in light grey and white plastic with very delicate raised panel detailing. A sprue of very brittle clear plastic is included, containing two canopies, open and closed, a head-up display glass panel and three landing-lights. Take great care when handling the canopies, as they are fragile. Their clarity also leaves a lot to be desired. A replacement vacform canopy can be found in Aeroclub's range.

Construction begins with the cockpit bathtub assembly. This comprises a floor, two side-walls with 'shelves' to represent the consoles, an instrument panel, rudder bar, control column and a front and rear coaming. The method of construction is rather sloppy, in that the side-walls have to be cemented to the floor with nothing to support them to ensure that they are vertical. In addition, the instrument panel and the coaming pieces have very little on which to locate, leaving the whole assembly rather wobbly until the cement dries.

The decals for the side consoles and instrument panel are best added after painting, but before constructing the bathtub. They must also be trimmed very close as they are somewhat oversize. There is a glaring error in the instruction sheet, which results in the bathtub being assembled back-to-front if the construction sequence is followed.

The bathtub sits on the moulded nosewheel well, which slopes down from front to rear, so the cockpit assembly should slope the same way, being deeper at the rear than at the front and not, as shown in the instructions, the other way round. The solution is to cement the side panels to the floor with the shallowest depth at the front, the top edge level and the floor sloping down from front to back. This also places the extensions to the shelves in the correct position on which to mount the instrument panel. The cutaway drawing B in the instruction sheet shows the correct layout.

A four-part KS–4 ejection seat is included in the kit which, while quite good, will benefit from being replaced with an Aeroclub white-metal Soviet ejection seat. Coincidentally, the white-metal seat provides just enough nose weight to prevent the model from being a tail-sitter.

FITTER-B. *(Model by author; photo by Tim Perry)*

Inserts for the bullet fairing in the nose and a jetpipe and afterburner are provided but, before adding them and cementing the fuselage halves together, I recommend that you drill out the prominent blow-off valve outlets located in the upper fuselage forward of the fin, and add the vanes from plastic card. These will enhance the appearance of the finished model considerably, although a study of photographs of SU–7s shows that these outlets are sometimes hidden by cover-plates when parked.

These covers can easily be depicted by rectangles of plastic card sanded to shape and painted red, which adds a dash of colour against a silver background. This method also provides a 'lazy' alternative to fabricating the vents. I compromised by having one blow-off valve covered and the other one added but with the cover casually left on top of the fuselage – again, as seen in photographs.

The suction-relief doors aft of the intake can also be opened out, although again, a careful perusal of photographs will show that these are sometimes open and sometimes not – I think it depends whether or not the engine is running.

With the cockpit bathtub and nose and jetpipe inserts in place, you can cement the fuselage halves together and when dry, clean them up. The long piping ducts on the fuselage are separate items, as is the nose ring, the latter requiring filler to blend it into the nose contours. The instructions show the nose-probe being added at this stage but this is best left off until the main construction is completed.

The wings are in upper and lower halves each side with acceptably thin trailing edges. The prominent wing fences, two per side, are integrally moulded, as are the wing-root cannon barrels and the port wing pitot boom. These latter two items are best removed and reapplied after you have completed painting. This is particularly true of the cannons which will look better if replaced with thin Contrail tube.

The wheel-wells have detail etched into the wing upper surface, but the shape of the well is incorrect when compared with photographs and scale drawings. The well should extend slightly into the fuselage but, because of the way the wing-root is moulded integrally with the fuselage, this detail is missing on the model. As a consequence, the maingear doors are also incorrect and should be remade in plastic card. A pair of clear landing-light lenses completes the wing construction.

The tailplane halves are in one piece with the tip anti-flutter

Sukhoi family, SU–11 FISHPOT-C, SU–7 FITTER-B and SU–22 FITTER-F, showing family lineage. *(Models by author; photo by Tim Perry)*

weight moulded integrally. These are more robust than the pitot and, with care can be left *in situ* during construction.

Once the wing-roots are blended in with filler and cleaned up, you can begin final detailing. No fewer than eight tiny intakes have to be added to the fuselage and wing-roots, as well as a larger overwing and two massive ventral intakes. These latter items will look better if reduced in size and reworked as they are 'lumpy' as moulded. Two under-fuselage and four wing pylons are added next, as is the undernose ILS aerial.

The nosewheel is moulded integrally with the leg but looks fine when cleaned up. The locating holes for the nose and maingear legs are very shallow, so I super-glued them in place for added strength. After having 'flats' filed on them, I added the mainwheels, again with super-glue, as the stub axles onto which they are mounted do not make for strong joints. The addition of main and nosewheel doors completes the assembly. Various underwing stores are provided, comprising the almost mandatory under-fuselage drop tanks, two further drop tanks for the wings as well as two 57mm 16-round rocket pods, two 5-round rocket pods, two low-drag and two older-style bombs.

With the windscreen cemented in place and masked off, the cockpit was packed with tissue and the wheels covered in cling-film to protect them. The model was airbrushed with Humbrol Polished Aluminium, followed by a coat of SNJ Spray Metal. The model was then re-masked and the various panels buffed up with the aluminium powder to give a patchwork effect, so typical on a bare metal aircraft. The gun blast panels on the fuselage are a difficult shape to paint straight onto the model, so a piece of clear decal film was painted a dark silver colour and, by drawing round a template made from plastic card, two pear-shaped pieces of decal were cut and applied to the fuselage. The decals provided are very thin and, after mine curled up on themselves, were replaced with items from the spares box. One final detail not provided in the kit is the pitch and yaw vanes on the nose-probe. These were fabricated from tiny pieces of plastic card cemented in place with super-glue.

References
Sukhoi Fitters in Action
(Squadron/Signal Publications)
Air International   Apr 1981
Air International   Sep 1986

15 SUKHOI SU–9/11 FISHPOT

TYPE: SINGLE-SEAT ALL-WEATHER INTERCEPTOR

ARMAMENT: *(SU–9)* 4 × AA–1 Alkali Beam-riding AAMs
           (SU–11) 2 × AA–3 Anab SARH & IR AAMs

Using the same tailed-delta configuration as the MiG–21, the SU–9 FISHPOT-B used the fuselage, tailplanes, fin and engine of the SU–7 married to a 60 degree delta wing to produce the first single-seat all-weather interceptor to enter service with the Soviet air force. The nose radar was housed in a small conical radome and armament comprised four AA–1 Alkali beam-riding air-to-air missiles, the same as those fitted to the MiG–19PM Farmer. Entering service in 1958/59, the SU–9 was superseded by its derivative, the SU–11, in the early 60s. Designated Fishpot-C by NATO, the SU–11 featured a larger inlet and conical centrebody which housed a new radar coded Skip-Spin. Associated with this new radar were new missiles, Semi-Active Radar-Homing AA–3 Anabs, although the number carried was reduced to just two.

It is thought that only a few Fishpots remain in Soviet service, the type being superseded by the SU–15 Flagon.

Model
Modellers wishing to create a Fishpot currently have two options open to them. The earlier Fishpot-B can be modelled by combining the fuselage, fin and tailplanes from the KP SU–7 with scratch-built delta wings from plastic card. The brake-chute housing will have to be removed from the base of the fin and the main undercarriage modified, although the legs and wheels can be used providing the 'skis' are removed. The nosewheel and doors will have to be obtained from the spares box as the SU–9 nosewheel is of a smaller diameter than the low-pressure SU–7 example.

The only 1:72 scale kits available are the vacforms produced by the Bristol firm of Gerald Elliott, both SU–9 and SU–11 variants being produced. While the basic shapes are correct, a great deal of work is required to produce a reasonable replica of the Fishpot, as the kits are fairly crude and lack detail. The kits suffer from being

Gerald Elliott vacform SU-11 FISHPOT-C with PP ladder. (*Model by author; photo by Tim Perry*)

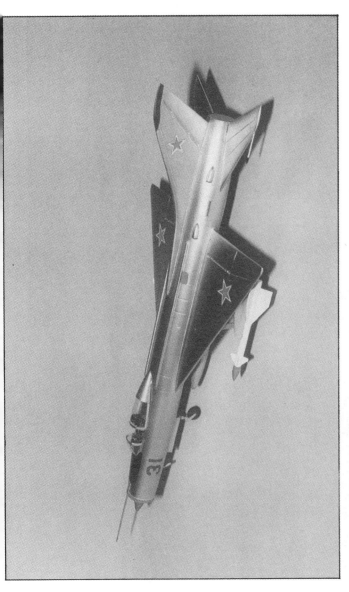

Note covers at nose, tail, on intakes and over exhaust louvres to avoid detailing these areas! *(Model by author; photo by Tim Perry)*

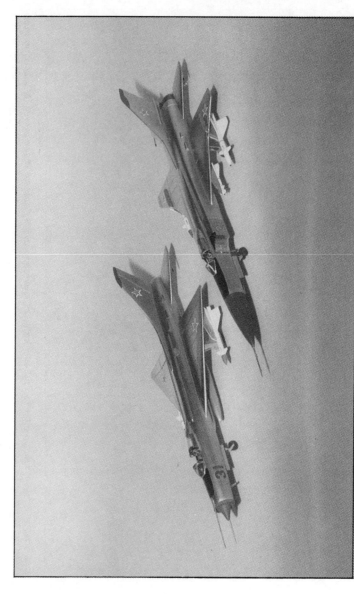

Sukhoi deltas, SU–11 FISHPOT and SU–15/21 FLAGON, illustrating family development. (*Models by author; photo by Tim Perry*)

packaged in a common box with an instruction sheet which covers the whole SU–7/9/11 family, the only concession to individuality being a half-plan of a SU–9/11.

Included amongst the kit releases announced for 1990 are examples of the SU–9 and SU–11 from Pioneer. Meanwhile, Gerald Elliot's SU–11 kit comprises three sheets of fairly thin plastic card, a bag of white-metal accessories and a clear canopy. The fuselage consists of two vertically split halves which, after rubbing down, had the cockpit and nosewheel well cut-outs removed. The nose intake and jetpipes were not opened up, as no interior detail is supplied; the white-metal nosecone which is supplied is far too short to be of any use. I decided to 'cheat' and depict the model with covers over the intake and tailpipe, which neatly sidesteps the problem. A white-metal seat of sorts is supplied but is best replaced, as are the bulkhead/instrument panel and the two rectangular consoles. In fact, the cockpit and nosewheel bay will need to be totally scratch-built in plastic card to achieve a reasonable effect.

Wings and tailplane are in upper and lower halves either side. The mainwheel wells need to be cut out from the lower wing halves before assembly, and spars made from plastic rod can be inserted through the fuselage to give some strength to the wing/fuselage joint. A lot of filler was required to blend in the wing-roots and the tailplanes needed to have their roots trimmed for a reasonable fit. Anti-flutter weights from plastic rod were added to the tailplane tips, and wing pylons from suitably shaped plastic card were added to the underside of the wings, outboard of the wheel-wells.

The white-metal main legs were affixed in place using super-glue and the white-metal mainwheels, which are in two halves, were cemented together before being super-glued to the legs. Maingear doors were cut from thin plastic card, their shape being arrived at by studying photographs, as no details are given on the instruction sheet. The nosewheel, also in white-metal, was unusable, being badly cast, so a replacement was found in the spares box.

The two prominent ducts on the upper fuselage were added, and a nosecone from a BAe Lightning kit was cemented in place with a thin ring of plastic card added to the intake lip to represent a blanking plate, the same effect being achieved at the rear end with a plastic card disc and ring. Nose-probe and wing-mounted pitot were added from tapered plastic rod and the under-fuselage drop tanks, although supplied in the kit, were obtained from a KP SU–7. The supplied cockpit canopy was rubbed down and separated into two parts before being cemented in place after the model was painted.

With the wheels covered in cling-film, and the nosecone and cockpit masked, the model was airbrused with Humbrol Metalcote Polished Aluminium which served as an undercoat for a final airbrushed coat of SNJ Spray Metal. This allowed the various panels to be masked and buffed up to achieve the patchwork effect so necessary on bare-metal aircraft.

The fin tip dielectric panel was painted dark grey and the nose and tail blanking plates bright red, which makes a nice contrast to the all-silver finish. One further detail which is missing from the kit is the pair of prominent exhuast vents in the upper fuselage forward of the fin. These vents should really be cut out and have louvres added from plastic card to be strictly accurate but, as my aircraft was being depicted 'closed down', with blanking plates in place, the vents were covered with rectangles of plastic card painted red to represent the covers seen in some photographs.

Scratch-built Anabs were added before the decals were applied. These consisted of the usual white-bordered red stars and two-digit code in blue on either side of the nose.

References
HCG   p149
Observers   p206

16 SUKHOI SU–15/21 FLAGON

TYPE: *SINGLE-SEAT ALL-WEATHER INTERCEPTOR*

ARMAMENT: *2 × AA–3 Anab AAMs in both radar guided and infra-red versions plus 2 × AA–8 Aphid short-range IR AMMs or 2 × GSh–23 twin-barrelled 23mm cannon pods on under-fuselage pylons*

First displayed to Western observers at a Soviet Aviation Day flypast in 1967, the SU–15 FLAGON bears a family resemblance to the SU–9/11 series, utilising the same wing and tail unit married to a twin-engined fuselage, with side-mounted intakes and a large nose-mounted radome. Powered by two 13,600lb Tumansky R–11F afterburning turbojets, the initial production version, Flagon-A, featured a straight delta wing and a conical radome. Flagon-B was a purely experimental STOL derivative and Flagon-C is a two-seat trainer variant of A.

The next major production version, Flagon-D, introduced a cranked wing leading edge, while Flagon-E was further modified, with a reportedly greater span wing and twin nosewheels. The final single-seat version is Flagon-F, which has an ogival-shaped radome replacing the conical shape of Flagon-E. This latest version is also designated SU–21, according to some publications. Flagon-G is a two-seat trainer version of F. One thing that is not explained in any of the publications I referred to is the fitment or otherwise of two large cooling intakes on the top rear fuselage either side of the fin. These are seen on some photographs but not on others, and appear on aircraft with and without ogival radomes.

It is not known whether these scoops are on an earlier-engined version, which has been retro-fitted with an ogival radome so that it looks like a Flagon-F, but it would seem to indicate that the F has been re-engined, which bears out the redesignation of SU–21.

Although being replaced in Soviet service with more up-to-date types such as the Fulcrum and Flanker, the SU–15/21 still soldiers on, although in diminishing numbers.

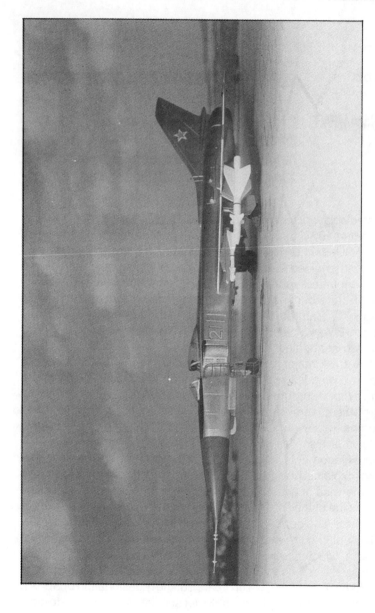

Pioneer SU–15/21 FLAGON-F with PP ladder and chocks. *(Model by author; photo by Tim Perry)*

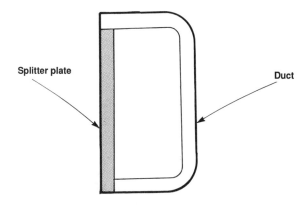

Splitter plate

Duct

Fig. 3 Correct method of attaching splitter plate

Model

The only 1:72 scale injection moulded kit of the Flagon is a recent release by a young company, Pioneer of Yorkshire, England. Fortunately, it is a reasonably accurate example and represents the latest variant, the SU–21 Flagon-F. It comes in a rather flimsy cardboard box, which will not endear it to stockists, but it features an excellent boxtop drawing by Don Greer of Squadron/Signal fame.

The kit consists of just 47 parts moulded in dark grey plastic, with fine etched panel detail plus a rather thick cockpit canopy. The latter item can be replaced with an Aeroclub vacform example intended for the SU–7, as it is the same style. Cockpit detail is sparse, consisting of just a floor and an armchair and cries out for additional work. Side consoles, instrument panel, control column and an Aeroclub white-metal seat can all be added to fill the 'office'.

The fuselage is in two halves, including the radome, and features a large cutout on the underside for the wing centre-section, while the wing is in three pieces, two upper halves and a one-piece lower section. Fin and tailplanes are single mouldings, the latter with their distinctive anti-flutter weights. These weights are moulded in line with the tailplane leading edge, whereas they should be pointing slightly upwards. Depict this on the model by gently bending them upwards until they are approximately 25 degrees from the horizontal and sand their tips to a more pointed profile.

The intakes are in two parts on either side, a splitter plate and the outer duct and it is in this area that the kit is slightly inaccurate. Head-on photographs of the Flagon show the intakes to be canted slightly inwards at their bottom edges and not mounted vertically as depicted by Pioneer. Not a major flaw, but one that I corrected by first cementing the splitter plate as shown in Fig. 3. (Incidentally, the exact method of location is not made clear in the instructions – don't try to fit the splitter plate *inside* the duct as I did at first.)

The wedge-shaped boundary-layer spill duct, which is moulded on the fuselage side, should have its bottom half scraped and sanded away so that the intake now fits closer to the fuselage at its bottom edge and adopts a canted-in position when cemented in place. The rear edge of the duct will not now match the contours of the fuselage, but this can be remedied by careful sanding and filling. Fig. 4 shows the method.

The rest of the construction is fairly straightforward. The lower wing section is cemented to the fuselage and then the two upper wing halves are attached, this sequence ensuring the minimum of filling at the wing-root. Main and nosewheels are cemented to their respective legs, legs and doors to the airframe and the undernose aerial and nose-probe fitted, after which the model is complete, apart from its armament.

This consists of two radar guided and two infra-red AA–3 Anab medium range missiles, each of which comprises three parts, fuselage with integrally moulded forward fins and horizontal tail surfaces plus the two vertical tail surfaces. Dimensions appear to

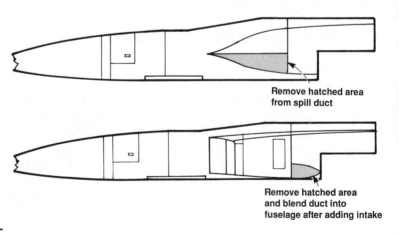

Remove hatched area
from spill duct

Remove hatched area
and blend duct into
fuselage after adding intake

Fig. 4 Method of altering intake angle

FLAGON-F with modified intakes. *(Model by author; photo by Tim Perry)*

be correct, although the flying surfaces are rather thick. These can be replaced from plastic card or, as I did, sanded down to a thinner section.

Four wing pylons are provided, but the instruction sheet shows them mounted the wrong way round – the deeper pylons parts 25 & 26 should be fitted outboard and the shallow ones parts 42 & 43 are fitted to the inner wing. The three-view drawing on the rear of the box and the front painting both depict the Flagon armed with all *four* Anabs, although all the published photographs I have seen show a mix of two Anabs – IR version on the outer port pylon and SARH version on the starboard – *plus* either two AA–8 Aphids on the inner wing pylons *or* two GSh–23 gun-pods on the fuselage pylons.

Only one colour scheme is catered for on the decal sheet – a natural metal example, for which six stars and a two-digit code are supplied. I sprayed my model with Humbrol Metalcote Polished Aluminium followed by a coat of airbrushed SNJ Spray Metal, which was then masked and buffed up. Markings came from the spares box. Some publications do have a drawing of a two-tone blue-grey camouflaged Flagon but, sadly, without photographic proof of such a scheme. One photo does show a camouflaged SU–21 and is captioned as being in tactical green and brown, but the photograph is not clear enough to discern the pattern.

References

HCG	p151
Observers	p208
Air International	Jan 1988
Warplane	No 84
Warplane	No 105

17 SUKHOI SU–17/20/22 FITTER C to K

TYPE: *SINGLE-SEAT VARIABLE-GEOMETRY CLOSE SUPPORT*

ARMAMENT: *2 × wing-root 30mm NR–30 cannon plus up to eight hardpoints for bombs, rockets, fuel tanks etc. up to an estimated 6,600lbs*

The SU–17/20/22 series represents a whole family of aircraft derived from the original SU–7 Fitter-B. To improve the modest tactical radius of action of the Fitter-B, the Sukhoi bureau added a variable-geometry wing with the pivots placed well outboard, which resulted in a large fixed section on which to hang the pylons without having to make them pivot. A small dorsal spine was added and the cockpit canopy was changed to a clamshell type, rather than the aft-sliding Fitter-Bs. With roughly the same dimensions as the SU–7, the SU–17 can carry more ordnance over a greater range and also has a better short-field performance.

The SU–17 Fitter-C entered Soviet service in 1970/71 and its export derivative, designated SU–20, was delivered to Poland in 1974. Fitter-D has an extended nose and large chin fairing housing a Doppler terrain-avoidance radar. Fitter-F is the export derivative of D, and Fitter-E is a two-seat trainer version of H. The next major variant is Fitter-H, with a longer and deeper nose section which is slightly drooped for improved forward visibility and an enlarged dorsal spine.

The fin is increased in height and squared off and a ventral fin has been added. This aircraft also incorporates a much improved avionics suite with a Laser Target Designator System mounted in the nose centrebody, radio altimeter and Doppler panels in the nose and a fire control computer. Later aircraft feature an additional pylon between the wing-root pylon and the outboard pylon. Fitter-G is a two-seat variant of H.

Fitter-J is an export version of H with a less capable avionics fit and re-engined with a Tumansky R–29 B, as fitted to the MiG–23/27 family.

The latest member of the Fitter family is the SU–22M–4 Fitter-K

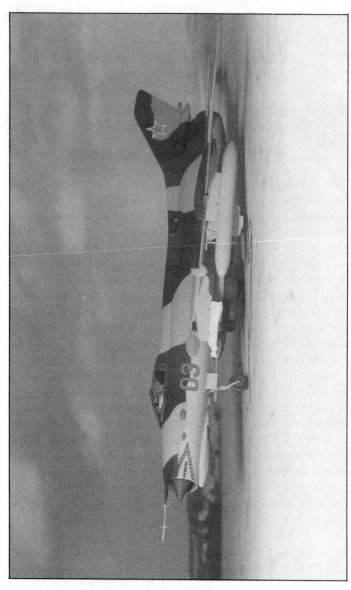

Hobbycraft SU–22 FITTER-F. Note decal film gun blast panel and map in cockpit from pocket diary. (*Model by author; photo by Tim Perry*)

which differs visually from H in having a ram-air intake located on the dorsal spine.

Model

There are currently four kits of the Fitter-C to K family in 1:72 scale – two injection moulded and two vacforms. The first, from Hobbycraft of Canada, depicts a SU–22 Fitter-F single-seater. Although generally reasonable in outline, this kit suffers from a number of niggling faults, not least of which is the box artwork and instruction sheet. Indeed this latter item seems to have been drawn by a five-year old, such is its crudity.

Turning to the kit itself, the fuselage has a strange 'waisted' section in the area of the jetpipe which needs to be eliminated. The cockpit detail consists of a moulded-in floor and rear bulkhead to which is added an instrument panel and seat, the latter item being best replaced with a white-metal example. Wings are in four sections either side and provision is made for the wings to pivot – although not in unison! The moulded-on wing fences will benefit from being thinned down.

Tailplanes are in upper and lower halves, left and right, and need the addition of anti-flutter weights made from plastic rod, at their tips. It is in the area of the undercarriage that the kit is badly let down. The items supplied are virtually useless, with the levered-suspension main legs being totally wrong, while the noseleg is a caricature. The wheels look like doughnuts and the whole offering is best consigned to the dustbin and replaced with items from the spares box, or scratch-built. If your pocket can afford it, substitute the undercarriage from a KP SU–7, although this is an expensive solution. Mount the mainwheels further outboard at the outer extremities of the wheel wells.

The rest of the kit is acceptable, consisting of two drop tanks, two AA–2 Atolls and their pylons, plus two further pylons. Additional armament can be obtained from the KP kit. Two very neatly moulded nose-probes are included, as is a clear, if somewhat thick, cockpit canopy. Markings are given for a camouflaged Libyan machine, for which a simple decal sheet, consisting of six green roundels, two rectangular green fin flashes and two intake warning triangles, is supplied.

The second offering from Hobbycraft is a SU–22U Fitter-E two-seat trainer version of Fitter-H. This kit is exactly the same as the earlier offering, apart from a new fuselage moulding for the two-seater, the addition of a further ejection seat and a revised tandem canopy. Much the same comments apply to this kit, although the decal sheet supplied is rather more comprehensive, consisting of six stars, intake warning triangles, two sets of numerals 0–9 in blue and a neat rendering of the Sukhoi house logo.

I'm not sure whether this aircraft actually exists. There is a drawing of a Fitter-E in *Air International* for April 1981, with the aft fuselage of a Fitter-F and the forward fuselage of the SU–7MK Moujik two-seater, which matches the Hobbycraft kit. However the September 1986 edition of the same magazine has the drawing of the Fitter-E revised, showing it with a larger dorsal spine, drooped nose and no step in the canopy line. This is exactly the same as Fitter-G, but with a shorter fin.

If the aircraft depicted in this kit does exist, then it is a reasonable model. If not, then I suppose the two-seat canopy and spine could be grafted on to a KP SU–7 to produce a SU–7 Moujik trainer and the swing-wings added to another SU–7 to create the prototype SU–7IG Fitter-B, so something can be salvaged from the kit.

So much for the injection-moulded kits. The vacforms available are a rendering of a Fitter-K by Gerald Elliott and an excellent kit from the Hungarian firm of PLANES which can be completed as either a Fitter-H or K, or their two-seat derivative, Fitter-G.

Taking the Gerald Elliott version first, this is reasonably accurate in outline, but suffers from a lack of detail. The fuselage consists of two halves in rather thin plastic card. A plastic-card bulkhead is supplied for the nose intake, as is a white-metal nosecone, although this was missing from my kit. If this item is anything like the example in the same company's SU–11 kit, then it is best replaced from the spares box. The only concession to accuracy at the rear end is a bulkhead – there is no jetpipe detail. The cockpit and nosewheel well need to be cut out and detail added from plastic card. A white-metal bulkhead/instrument panel and two side consoles are supplied, but are best replaced with plastic card. The white-metal ejection seat, which looks remarkably like a Martin-Baker design and is common to all Gerald Elliott kits of Soviet aircraft, can be replaced with an Aeroclub item.

The wings are in four pieces either side, while the tailplanes are in upper and lower halves left and right. The latter items require the addition of anti-flutter weights at their tips. The cockpit canopy is in clear acetate but is rather cloudy. The main undercarriage legs are in white-metal, as is the noseleg and wheel, although once again this is rendered useless by being badly cast. No such problem applies to the mainwheels, which are cast in two halves, thereby eliminating the 'step' which afflicts the nosewheel. Pylons

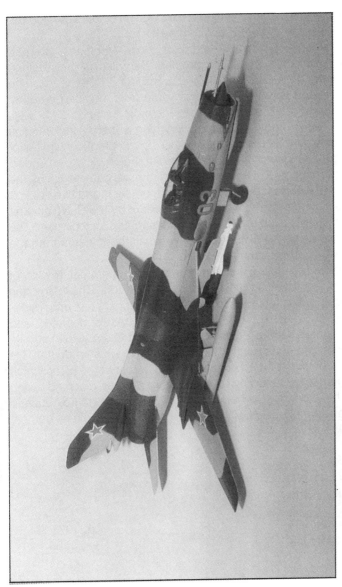

FITTER-F. Red painted bulges, which are moulded onto aircraft's nose, are actually covers over the AOA and air-data sensors. These should be removed and replaced with PP Aeroparts items if the aircraft is depicted 'on the move'. (*Model by author; photo by Tim Perry*)

and wing fences are separate items, while underwing stores are confined to four drop tanks, two under the fuselage and two on the outboard wing pylons. The instruction sheet features a three-view drawing of a camouflaged K although no colours are quoted, nor are any decals supplied with the kit.

The second vacform is a much more ambitious attempt, although availability might be a problem. Samples can be obtained either direct from the manufacturer or through PP Aeroparts, who have a limited supply. The Planes vacform is moulded in rather 'soapy' plastic, although it is reasonably stout and sands well. Detail is rather 'fiddly' although everything is there – including all the pylons, various small intakes, nosecone, complete with Laser Designator window, wheels, two styles of drop tank and an under-fuselage recce pod. The different versions are catered for by the addition of inserts for the ram-air intake on the K and two cockpit canopies, single for the J and K and tandem for the G. No cockpit detail is supplied, so modellers will have to furnish their own. The same applies to the undercarriage legs, although items from the KP SU–7 could be used here.

Construction follows much the same pattern as the other vacform, but there is much more detail in this kit. The instruction sheet comprises four-view drawings of a Hungarian H with a side-view of a Soviet K, with camouflage schemes depicted and colours noted. Scrap views of the two-seat G are also included, but it is in the construction drawing that the kit is let down. This consists of an exploded diagram in one corner of the plans which is altogether too 'fiddly' to be of any use – a larger, clearer drawing would have been more helpful. Markings will have to be obtained from the spares box as will any offensive stores – rockets, bombs, missiles etc.

References
Sukhoi Fitters in Action
(Squadron/Signal Publications)

Air International	Apr 1981
Air International	Sep 1986

18 SUKHOI SU–24 FENCER

TYPE: *TWO-SEAT VARIABLE-GEOMETRY ALL-WEATHER INTERDICTION AND STRIKE*

ARMAMENT: *One, or possibly two, six-barrelled gatling type 30mm cannon plus up to approx. 17,500lbs of ordnance on four under-fuselage, two fixed-glove and two swivelling wing pylons*

Making its first flight around 1970, and entering squadron service in 1975, the SU–24 FENCER posed a new threat to NATO defence chiefs with its ability to strike at Western targets from bases within the Soviet Union. Designed to replace the Yak–28 Brewer, the Fencer has sufficient range to supersede the TU–16 Badger and TU–22 Blinder in the nuclear strike role as well as being a tactical bomber, reconnaissance aircraft and electronic warfare platform, although why it should be designated as a 'fighter' by the ASCC is a mystery. The crew of two are housed side-by-side under a split two-piece clamshell canopy.

Six variants of Fencer have been identified. Fencer-A had a squared-off rear fuselage while Fencer-B's rear end was 'dished' between the jetpipes, possibly indicating a change of engine type and has a larger brake-chute housing at the base of the fin. Fencer-C was the major service variant with revised and improved avionics, multiple nose-probes, ESM blisters on the intake trunks and upper fin and a cooling intake in the leading edge of the fin.

Fencer-D was the next variant to be identified, entering service in 1983. This features a longer nose, possibly with a new radar, increased chord on the leading edge of the lower fin giving a distinct 'kinked' appearance, large overwing fences on the fixed gloves which merge in with deeper, extended pylons and an electro-optical sensor aft of the nosewheel bay. The complex nose-probes are replaced with a single spike with pitch/yaw vanes and the aircraft has in-flight refuelling capability.

Fencer-E is thought to be a dedicated reconnaissance variant fitted with SLAR, IR linescan and optical cameras, and the

Gerald Elliott vacform SU–24 FENCER–C. This is an early attempt at a FENCER before much data was available. Mainwheel legs are incorrect. (*Model by author; photo by Tim Perry*)

designation Fencer-F is reserved for a dedicated electronic warfare version designed to replace 'Brewer-E' in this role.

Model

There are two 1:72 scale models of the Fencer known to me, and both of them are vacforms, by Gerald Elliott and Planes of Hungary. Taking the Gerald Elliott kit first, like most of the kits from this manufacturer, the offering appears to be accurate in outline, based on the latest available data, but needs a great deal of work to produce an acceptable model.

The kit represents the shorter nosed Fencer-C and has a vertically split fuselage with integrally moulded fin and rudder. The nose and mainwheel bays need to be opened up and boxed in, as does the cockpit. I added a central console and instrument panel from plastic card with white-metal Aeroclub ejection seats. The side-mounted intakes are moulded flush with the fuselage sides so, for scale appearance, they should be carefully cut off and splitter plates added from thin plastic card before the intakes are cemented back into place and cleaned up.

The intake on the fin leading edge was fashioned from plastic card as was the ram-air intake on the top of the fuselage. The rear fuselage around the jetpipes was completely recontoured by cutting away the underside, adding jetpipes from plastic tube and filling in the area between the pipes with Milliput shaped to give a 'dished' appearance. The two bulges under the forward fuselage which house the cannon and its ammunition were fashioned from spare bomb halves and Contrail tubing.

The swing-wings are in four halves on either side and were cemented to the fuselage in the forward swept position using a plastic rod spar for strength. The two-part tailplane halves were added and all the various detail applied. This consists of the ESM fairings on the intake trunks and fin tip shaped from scrap plastic, the four under-fuselage, and two wing pylons plus the two ventral fins from plastic card, and the nose-probes and pitots from scrap. The canopy was carefully removed from its backing, sanded down and cut into three sections with a razor saw before being cemented into place in the open position – note the unusual twin clamshell 'petals'. The kit-supplied drop tanks were added to scratch-built pylons and cemented in place on the wing glove. Photographic confirmation of any other type of underwing store has yet to be found.

The twin mainwheels came from the spares box and were attached to the white-metal legs with super-glue, and the noseleg

SU-24 FENCER. Note unusual split clamshell canopy. (*Model by author; photo by Tim Perry*)

was replaced with the twin wheels and mudguard from a MiG–23 kit. The aircraft is finished in the only scheme seen so far, mid-grey upper surfaces with white undersides, radome and wing, fin and tailplane leading edges. Markings consist of the usual red stars and a two-digit code applied to the intake sides.

The Planes vacform arrived on my desk as I was typing the final draft of this book, so I have not yet had the chance to build it. It represents the later Fencer-D variant with a longer nose and extended fin leading edge. It is moulded on two sheets of the usual 'soapy' plastic, with an excellent clear canopy.

The instruction sheet is much improved over previous releases, with a five-view drawing of a camouflaged Fencer in dark brown and sandy yellow upper surfaces and sky blue undersides. I have never seen a Fencer in this scheme but I have no reason to doubt Sandor Eses' data – indeed he quotes the scheme as being applied to a SU–24 MK in the south-east Soviet Union in the summer of 1989, so he must have some documentary proof!

The 'exploded' construction drawing is much clearer than that supplied with the same company's SU–22 Fitter, and there is a potted history of the type, in both Hungarian and English. Three rather smudgy photographs of SU–24s are also included.

The fuselage is divided into a horizontally split rear fuselage, which consists of four parts, upper and lower halves plus two inserts containing the lower fixed wing glove (the upper glove being integral with the upper fuselage section) and a vertically split forward fuselage complete with moulded-on boundary-layer diverter ramps. Intakes and splitter plates are provided, as is a bulkhead between the front and rear fuselage sections.

The vertical fin, tailplanes and each outer wing panel are in two halves, the wings having dog-teeth moulded into their roots should anyone want to attempt to make the wings pivot! No cockpit detail is provided, nor are there any undercarriage legs, although the wheels are supplied on the sheet. The modeller will have to scratch-build these areas as well as the undercarriage bays. All the weapons pylons are supplied, as well as two drop tanks, four AS–7 Kerry air-to-surface missiles, ten small practice bombs and four rocket pods, all of which are usable but could be replaced from the spares box. No decals are included but these can easily be obtained from other sources.

All in all, this is an excellent, accurate rendition of the latest Soviet offensive strike aircraft – I can't wait to start building it!

Who knows, with the surge in interest in all things Russian, maybe a company like Hasegawa might be persuaded to do for the Fencer what they have done for the F–111, now that sufficient data is available.

References
Air International   Sep 1987
Warplane   No 106

19 SUKHOI SU–25 FROGFOOT

TYPE: *SINGLE-SEAT CLOSE-SUPPORT*

ARMAMENT: *1 × GSh–23 23mm twin-barrel cannon plus 10 underwing stores pylons for an estimated 9,920lbs of ordnance*

Regarded as the Soviet equivalent of the American Fairchild A–10 Tankbuster, the FROGFOOT was first identified by US reconnaissance satellite at the Ramenskoye test centre in the late 1970s and was given the provisional designation RAM–J by the US Department of Defense. Delivered to the Frontal Aviation regiments in 1980, the SU–25 was allocated the NATO reporting name Frogfoot in 1982.

An extremely rugged aircraft, the Frogfoot's engines, non-afterburning Tumansky R–13–300s, can reportedly run on anything from diesel oil to lighter fluid! The pilot is protected by substantial amounts of armour in the cockpit structure, as well as a bullet-proof windscreen. The type saw service in Afghanistan, where many lessons were learned during its deployment in conjunction with Mil Mi–24 Hind helicopter gunships. This testing under operational conditions has, among other things, led to the fitment of additional flare dispensers along the top of the engine nacelles in addition to the internal fit at the base of the fin.

Model
There are currently three 1:72 scale injection-moulded kits of the Frogfoot – from KP, Revell and Hobbycraft.

Although I can't comment on the accuracy, or otherwise, of the Hobbycraft kit, the modeller faces a dilemma in choosing between the other two. The KP kit is the more accurate of the two and checks out well against the latest published plans. It is, however, not as well moulded as its Western counterpart, and lacks the finesse and delicacy of Revell's offering.

It consists of 88 parts moulded in light grey for the main components and white for all the rest, with fine raised panel detail. A clear sprue is provided, which contains a head-up display

KP SU–25 FROGFOOT with detailed cockpit, ladder, pylon sway braces and numerous aerials from PP Aeroparts' forthcoming SU–25 detail set. *(Model by author; photo by Tim Perry)*

screen, two wingtip landing-light lenses and, this is where it scores over the Revell kit, two canopies, both open and closed. Not only is an open option given, but the clamshell portion of the canopy includes the rear metal framework which opens with it. If the Revell canopy is depicted in the open position, not only will the windscreen need to be separated, but also the fuselage aft of the cockpit opening will need to be cut away and added to the rear of the clear canopy.

Ten parts go to make up the cockpit interior including a four-part ejection seat, while the fuselage consists of two vertically split halves with a cockpit coaming, rear armoured bulkhead and the prominent cover over the seat top. The engine nacelles are separate from the fuselage and are made up from two halves, into which are cemented inserts for the compressor faces and exhausts as well as intake rings and jetpipes, before the completed assemblies are added to the fuselage sides. Fin and tailplanes are all one-piece mouldings, as are the wings. All suffer from a certain 'lumpiness' as well as a considerable amount of flash. Nonetheless, they can be cleaned up with little difficulty.

Mainwheel legs are crude and the one-piece noseleg and wheel suffers from a flash problem, but again looks fine when cleaned up. Eight main pylons and two sets of alternative outer pylons are included and a large selection of underwing stores is provided including drop tanks, large and small bombs, rocket pods and two AA–8 Aphids. The instruction sheet is printed in Czech, German and English and includes a three-view drawing of the camouflage scheme for a Soviet machine, with Humbrol paint numbers being quoted. The box-art features a Czech machine on the front with a four-view on the reverse showing a different camouflage scheme.

Decals are supplied for the cockpit instrument panel and side consoles, as well as six Soviet stars and the same number of Czech roundels. Code numbers consist of white outlines 0–9 for the Soviet machine and black and white outlines for the Czech example. A host of stencil data is included on the sheet but, sadly, no details of placement are provided.

Turning to the Revell offering, this is moulded in brown plastic and features delicately engraved panel detail with detailed wheel bays, the area around the 23mm cannon being particularly well executed. The cockpit on this kit consists of a three-part seat which is cemented to a floor with moulded-in side consoles and a control column. An instrument panel and rear armoured bulkhead are added to the upper half of the *horizontally* split fuselage before the bottom half, complete with cockpit assembly, is

FROGFOOT with added flare dispensers over engine exhausts. (*Model by author; photo by Tim Perry*)

FROGFOOT on display at Paris salon. Note flare dispensers. (*Photo by Robin Howard*)

Note canopy stay, grab handle on fuselage behind cockpit, folding ladder, aerials and rear-view mirrors – all in PP's detail set. (*Photo by Robin Howard*)

cemented into place. The engine nacelles are moulded integrally with the upper and lower fuselage halves, while the laser nose is a separate part.

Revell seem to have a predeliction for shutters, for this kit features two of them which are meant to be cemented into the separate engine intake fronts, while the two flame-holders are attached to the separate exhaust nozzles. Incidentally, it is nice to see the parts named on the instruction sheet rather than just being numbered. It is informative and adds to the builder's knowledge of the aircraft – rather more than the usual 'cement part A to part B', and especially useful for the younger modeller.

Mainwheels and knuckle-jointed legs are good mouldings, while the nosewheel is attached to a two-part leg and separate mudguard.

While the fuselage checks out reasonably well against the available plans, the wings, which are moulded as an upper section with a lower insert, are grossly undersized, being 8mm short in span in 1:72 scale. Not only is the span too small, which could be corrected by the addition of plastic card to the tips, but the sweep of the outer panels is too great, resulting in the wing requiring the addition of plastic card to the outer leading edge as well as to the tip to bring the wing back to the correct dimensions – a not insurmountable task, but one which the modeller shouldn't have to undertake.

Having criticised the wing profile, I must say that the separate wingtip pods are real gems, featuring dive-brakes which may be cemented in the open or closed position, complete with tiny actuating rams. Also included are little landing-lights which should, of course, be left off if the undercarriage is depicted in the retracted position.

A host of underwing ordnance is supplied, including two drop tanks, two AS–7 Kerry air-to-surface missiles, two AA–8 Aphid IR air-to-air missiles, rocket pods and bombs on twin ejector racks. Fin and tailplanes are single-piece mouldings, while the twin nose-probes with pitch and yaw vanes, IFF and towel-rail aerials are all very delicately moulded. The clear cockpit canopy is a one-piece moulding, as mentioned previously.

The instruction sheet has a poorly drawn four-view of the Frogfoot showing the camouflage pattern and quoting FS numbers for the main colours. The small decal sheet contains six red stars and the usual two-digit code numbers in blue, plus six Czech roundels and a four-digit code in black.

Summing up, if you want an accurate Frogfoot with an open

canopy then choose the KP kit but, if you are prepared to forgo the accuracy and want a crisply-moulded kit with a closed cockpit canopy, then the Revell kit is for you.

PP Aeroparts are working on a detail set for the Frogfoot which will be similar to their MiG–21 set with retractable boarding ladder, aerials, sway-braces etc.

References

Air International	Jul 1986
Air International	May 1986
Air International	Sep 1989
Warplane	No 105

20 SUKHOI SU–27 FLANKER

TYPE: *SINGLE-SEAT INTERCEPTOR*

ARMAMENT: *1 × 30mm cannon and two pylons under the centre fuselage, two under the intake ducts and two on the inner wings for AA–10 Alamo long-range AAMs plus two outer wing and two wingtip pylons for AA–8 Aphid short-range IR AAMs*

The existence of the SU–27 was first revealed by the US Department of Defense in 1979, with the release of photographs taken by reconnaissance satellite of the Ramenskoye flight test centre, near Moscow. FLANKER entered flight tests in 1977 and was seen by the public in a Soviet television programme in 1985, although this example is believed to have been an early prototype.

This prototype, now designated Flanker-A by NATO, differed from the production Flanker-B in having rounded wingtips, vertical and horizontal tail surfaces mounted directly onto the rear engine/fuselage nacelles and a nosewheel leg with twin nosewheels

Revell SU–27 FLANKER – white areas are plastic card additions. Tailcone is phantom drop tank. (*Model by author; photo by Tim Perry*)

View showing modified wingtip pylons, new tailbooms and tailplane leading edges, new ventral fins, new wing roots and ESM aerials on intake trunks. (*Model by author; photo by Tim Perry*)

mounted in line with the cockpit windscreen, which retracted rearwards into a bay beneath the canopy. It was in this configuration that most early speculative drawings of the Flanker appeared in the Western press.

Entering service in 1986, the true layout of the production version, Flanker-B was revealed during intercepts by Royal Norwegian Air Force aircraft over the Baltic. Then, on 13 September 1987, an overly enthusiastic Flanker pilot afforded the photographer of a RNoAF P–3B Orion the opportunity to take close-up shots of his aircraft when he flew in close formation with the Orion – so close, in fact, that his port fin tip collided with the Orion's starboard outer propeller!

Flanker-B differs from the prototype Flanker-A in a number of respects. The rounded wingtips have given way to squared-off tips, sporting launch rails for self-defence missiles, possibly AA–8 Aphids. The rear end has been drastically altered, the fins and tailplanes are now mounted on booms separate from the engines in the manner of the F–15 and the inter-nozzle fairing has been extended rearwards by approx. 4.25ft and is now a distinctive cylindrical body fairing, possibly containing fuel and a brake parachute.

Twin ventral fins are mounted beneath the booms and the nosewheel leg has been moved aft, retracts forward and is fitted with a single nosewheel, enclosed at the rear by a mudguard to prevent foreign object damage to the engines.

Model

Modellers wishing to create a miniature Flanker currently have two choices – an excellent Hungarian vacform by Planes or a drastically inaccurate injection-moulded sample from Revell. Airfix/ Heller have announced releases of kits of this fighter in 1990 in both single- and two-seat versions, but it remains to be seen how accurate they are. No doubt other manufacturers will attempt a version.

The vacform kit consists of two sheets of fairly thick plastic card with nicely engraved panel detail. Everything is included on the sheets; wheels, pylons, 5 AA–10 Alamos, 2 AA–8 Aphids and an unidentified missile which might be some sort of ECM pod. Even the nosewheel mudguard is moulded. The accompanying instruction sheet includes an accurate four-view drawing with camouflage and marking detail, but the exploded construction diagram is rather 'crowded' and difficult to read. No cockpit detail is provided, so it is left to the modeller to scratch-build an interior using the latest photographs from the Paris Salon as a guide.

Construction is fairly straightforward, although the way the deep recesses around the engine exhausts have been moulded does not allow the upper and lower fuselage halves to be laid flat for

Extended nosewheel bay. (*Model by author; photo by Tim Perry*)

sanding, so much scraping is called for. A beautifully-moulded, clear canopy is included, complete with infra-red search and track ball in front of the windscreen. Although the wheels are moulded, the legs will have to be scratch-built from plastic rod and tube. The same comment applies to the missiles, unless you are prepared to cut out and sand down the supplied items.

Sandor Eses, the man behind Planes, has recently released a completely new vacformed nose section, canopy and taller vertical fins for the SU–27B two-seater which can be grafted on to the original vacform. Supplies of this very accurate vacform are somewhat sporadic but samples may be obtained via PP Aeroparts.

Turning to the Revell injection-moulded kit, I wrote an article for *Scale Models* on converting this basically inaccurate model into something approaching a reasonable likeness to a SU–27. The article was written before the Flanker's appearance at the 1989 Paris Salon and is reproduced here, suitably amended in the light of the Paris data.

Fuselage (Lower)

The nosewheel bay moulded into the lower fuselage (part A2) needs to be extended by 12mm. This is done by carefully sawing through the rear vertical wall of the bay and cutting out an extension, the full width of the bay. A further extension, which houses the retraction stay, is made by removing the forward portion of the moulded fairing to leave a rectangular slot 16mm long by 4mm wide. The removed fairing should be retained, as it

Heavily modified Revell FLANKER with PP Aeroparts' new SU–27 ladder. (*Model by author; photo by Tim Perry*)

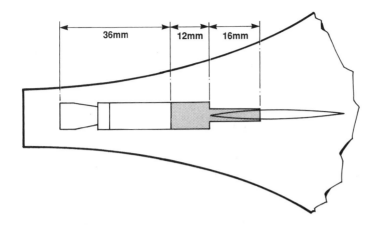

Fig. 5 Remove hatched area

is later attached to the rear stay of the nosewheel leg to form a door.

Box in the rear of the new bay with plastic card and add detail. Use the kit part B27 forward door and the front 4mm cut from kit part A10 to close off the forward portion of the existing under-carriage bay and fair in with filler. The nosewheel bay should now start 18mm from the front of the kit part A2 and extend 32mm rearwards, with a further 16mm bay for the retraction jack. Fig. 5 refers.

The bullet fairing at the rear end of the lower fuselage is removed and the resultant gap filled with plastic card.

The next step was not done on my model until the upper and lower fuselage halves were cemented together and the rear fairing had been added, but in retrospect it is better done at this stage. When comparing the Revell fuselage in profile with drawings, the kit was too high at the rear end and didn't have the distinct curved shape of the original.

To correct this, the rear end on the kit needs to be bent down-wards by about 20mm. Start this alteration by sawing completely through the lower fuselage where the compressor faces are mounted and put aside until later.

Fuselage (Upper)
This first step appears drastic but is not too heart-stopping and results in a better profile shape to the fuselage.

Locate the moulded panel line across the upper fuselage which is 18mm to the rear of the air brake housing and *carefully* bend the rear end downwards. It may help to cut two V-shaped notches at the wing-roots and score across the inside of the fuselage to relieve the stress. Remove the rear bullet fairing and fill in the gap. Drill a hole in the starboard cannon trough and add a muzzle from the inside made from Contrail tubing, protruding 2mm into the trough.

The appearance of the cannon can also be improved by rubbing down the fairing over the muzzle to reduce its height.

If the canopy is to be depicted in the open position, remove the hatched cover from the rear of the cockpit opening and put aside until later. Photographs show this portion attached to the underside of the canopy and opening with it.

Complete the cockpit assembly and add detail as desired. I left out the seat, replacing it later with a white-metal Soviet ejection seat. I also added detail to the rather bare area behind the seat to represent the various 'black-boxes'.

Cement the forward portion of the lower fuselage to the upper and, when the assembly is thoroughly dry, add the rear portion after first shaving off some plastic from the front faces of the engine nacelles to compensate for the increased rake of the upper fuselage. Don't forget to add the compressor faces before cementing the lower fuselage in place!!

Nosecone

The most obvious error in the Revell kit is the nosecone, which is too bulbous and is mounted too high, giving a chin-up appear-

Revell FLANKER – tail logo is incorrect. (*Model by author; photo by Tim Perry*)

Revell FLANKER. (*Model by author; photo by Tim Perry*)

ance, which does not re-create the distinct nose-down profile of the Flanker. Correct this by first adding two discs of plastic card, one to the front opening of the fuselage and one to the rear of the nosecone. Plastic card packing is then added to the upper half of the nosecone disc, which allows the nosecone to be mounted with its bottom edge butting up against the fuselage but with the upper edge mounted further forward, thereby tilting the whole nose forward. Once the cement is thoroughly dry all the gaps around the upper nose area should be filled with plastic card and filler. The nosecone is now mounted at the correct angle when viewed from the side – see Fig. 6 – but is still not the right shape at its front end.

Remedy this by applying Milliput and shaping to the correct profile, using the drawing as a guide. Try to achieve the right shape before the Milliput sets as this will save a lot of sanding later on.

Intakes
Having provided two nicely detailed compressor faces for the

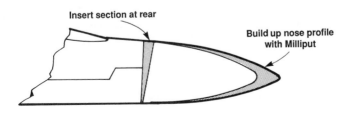

Insert section at rear

Build up nose profile with Milliput

Fig. 6 Insert section at rear and build up nose profile with Milliput

Planes vacform SU–27 FLANKER with PP ladder, and Warpac pilot and groundcrew. (*Model by author; photo by Tim Perry*)

intake trunking in the lower fuselage, Revell then hide them with a curious shutter arrangement fitted to the front of the intakes!!

In fact the Flanker's FOD protection system consists of a mesh grid, hinged at the rear, which slopes forward from bottom to top when deployed and lies flush with the bottom of the intake trunking when retracted. It is better to leave these shutters off and remove the moulded location ledges, as well as thinning down the leading

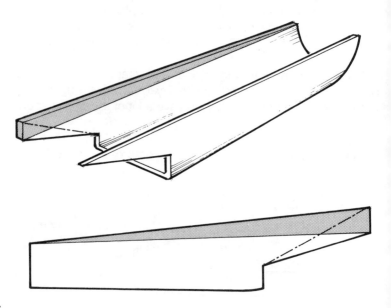

Fig. 7 Deepen engine intakes

Planes FLANKER – most accurate kit to date. (*Model by author; photo by Tim Perry*)

edges of the ramps and rounding off their lower lips to give a better scale appearance.

The intakes themselves are too shallow in side view and are canted outwards too far. Remedy this fault by cementing a thin triangular sliver of plastic card to the top edge of the *outer* walls of each intake – parts B9 & B19 – and when set, carefully cut the intake lip back to a steeper angle to match the inner face. This has the effect of deepening the intake and forcing it inwards – you will have to twist it along its length to get it to fit at its rear end – see Fig. 7.

Cement the intakes in place and fair in their rear ends with filler. Complete the work on the fuselage by adding a new extended tailcone between the jetpipes. Mine was made from a 1:72 scale Phantom wing drop tank, which is the right diameter and shape. Modify the front end of the upper half of the drop tank to fair into the fuselage spine, shorten the lower half and blend in the whole assembly with Milliput.

The strakes on either side of the tailcone are new additions first seen at Paris and terminate in what looks like some sort of ECM fit. These strakes can be fashioned from plastic card added to the sides of the tailcone and carved to shape.

Wings

According to most references, the leading edge sweep on the Flanker is given as 40 degrees while Revell depict the wings swept at 45 degrees. The Revell wings are modified by removing a section from the wingtip and inserting a triangular piece of plastic card at the wing-roots to rotate the leading edge through the necessary 5 degrees – see Fig. 8.

The trailing edge protrusions and the underside fairings were removed and the plastic card wing-roots sanded to airfoil section. The leading-edge slats and the flaps and ailerons will need to be re-scribed, but do not cement the wings into place at this stage.

Fuselage rear end

The Revell kit's tailplane is mounted too high and is in line with the wings. Drawings and photographs show it to be mounted lower down relative to the wings and the booms onto which the fins and tailplanes are mounted is lower than depicted in the kit. The remedy again calls for some drastic sawing and rearranging.

Remove the kit booms by sawing along a line adjacent to the engine nacelles, forward to a point 4cm from the rear face of the nacelles.

Fill in the resultant gap in the engine nacelles with plastic card

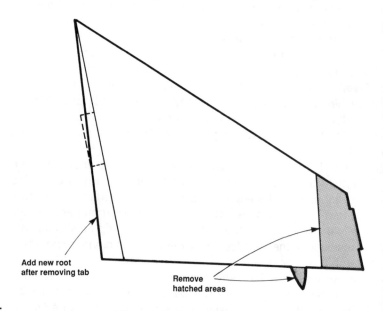

Add new root after removing tab

Remove hatched areas

Fig. 8 Remove hatched area and add new root after removing tab

and blend in with filler. Refer to Fig. 9 and make new booms from plastic card consisting of lower piece A, mounted so that its rear tip is positioned just below the centreline of the engine exhaust when viewed from the side. A filler, piece B, is used to fair in the upper section of the boom and a new mount for the fin, piece C, is shaped and cemented vertically onto the boom. The sketch, Fig. 10, illustrates the method.

Blend in the new booms with generous amounts of filler.

Fins

The kit fins can now be improved by removing the lower 9mm – Fig. 11 – and adding the leading-edge intakes at the fin roots. Mine were made by taking a section of Contrail tubing, cutting it to length and squeezing it to an oval section before cementing it into a slot cut into the fin. Fair in the new intakes with filler and mount the fins onto the new booms, making sure that they are vertical when viewed from the front.

The kit ventral fins are undersize and are best replaced with new ones made from plastic card.

Tailpanes

Once again the kit items need to be altered. They appear to be the right shape but they are too small in chord. Remove a section from their leading edges to give flat mating surfaces and add extensions from plastic card cemented in place with super-glue for strength. Blend in with filler and sand to airfoil section.

That completes all the major alterations to the kit, so the wings, tailplanes and ventral fins can now be added. I inserted short lengths of plastic rod into all the parts before cementing to provide some strength to the joints. Once all the parts are firmly in place and the joints filled and sanded smooth, the whole model should be given a thorough clean-up in soapy water to remove all the dust

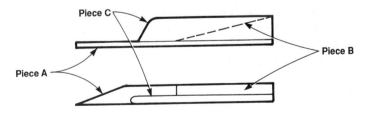

Fig. 9 Starboard boom

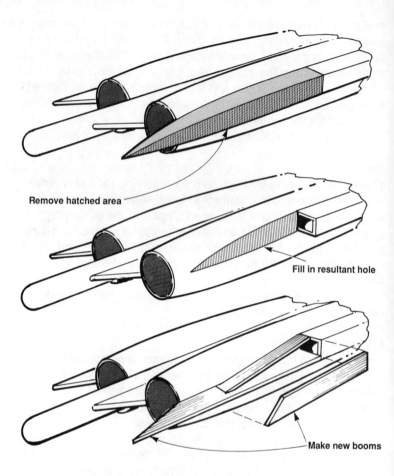

Remove hatched area

Fill in resultant hole

Make new booms

Fig. 10 Remove hatched area, fill in resultant hole and make new booms

from the sawing and sanding. When dry a quick coat of light grey primer will show up any areas in need of further work. It is important that any conversion work carried out should be invisible and all new sections should blend in totally, particularly around the nose and wing-roots.

Final detailing

The various fin trailing edge antennas were added from suitably shaped rod and the nose-mounted pitot was made from a short length cut from a pin inserted into a length of tube, the whole lot being cemented into a hole drilled into the nose. The assembly was then faired into the nosecone with filler. The kit windscreen can be utilised but the offset fairing for the IR sensor needs to be removed and the rake of the windscreen should be reduced by first removing plastic from the rear lower corner and then sanding it flat so that it seats correctly onto the cockpit coaming. Add a new IR sensor made from scrap clear sprue and blend into the windscreen with filler. The main canopy is useless – it is the wrong shape and looks totally inaccurate. I replaced it with a spare canopy from an old Airfix F–15 Eagle which is the right shape, but needs a section removing from the rear end to fit properly. The canopy was mounted in the open position to hide any slight discrepancies in fit.

The mainwheels from the kit are used without modification, but the nosegear leg will need to be replaced either by scratch-building from rod and tube or by utilising the kit upper leg super-glued to a new front fork from the spares box. Note that there are the three prominent landing-lights on the noseleg. The single nosewheel came from the spares box, but I still haven't found a method of reproducing a realistic stoneguard. Mainwheel doors with their rectangular tabs removed can be used but a new nosewheel door will have to be made from plastic card. The fairing for the retraction stay, which was removed earlier, can now be added. Parts B15 and B16, which were thought to be camera fairings do, in fact, contain some sort of retractable arm which

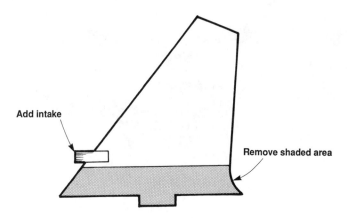

Fig. 11 Remove shaded area and add intake

Side-by-side view of modified Revell and Planes FLANKERS. (*Models by author; photo by Tim Perry*)

extends and locks into the mainwheel leg. This can just be discerned on some close-up photographs of the Flanker. The two ECM aerial fairings, parts B17 and B18 are too small and are best replaced with scratch-built items. The kit part B33 is a mystery and was left off. The wingtip fairings from the kit are replaced by scratch-built items and the pylons can be modified to accord with the latest drawings. The upper fuselage intake spill doors moulded by Revell are completely fictitious so they need to be filled in.

Revell and Planes FLANKERS. (*Models by author; photo by Tim Perry*)

FLANKER at Paris salon. Note flap, intake on fin leading edge, new Sukhoi logo on fin and locking pin on maingear leg. (*Photo by Robin Howard*)

Two-seater SU–27UB at Paris. Note increased area of gun-blast panel, rear-view mirrors and scuffed Paris buzz number. (*Photo by Robin Howard*)

FLANKER tailcone with white ESM aerials. (*Photo by Robin Howard*)

The Flanker displayed at Paris did not have weapons pylons, nor underwing armament, so I left these items off the Revell model. If a weapons fit is required the AA–10 Alamo missiles will have to be scratch-built, the items supplied by Revell do not bear any resemblance to the real thing. I fitted my vacform version with six Alamos, 2 AA–A10A Alamo-A short-burn SAR homing missiles in tandem under the fuselage, 2 AA–10B Alamo-B short-burn IR homing missiles on the inner wing pylons and 2 AA–10C long-burn SAR homing missiles mounted one under each intake trunk. The missiles were scratch-built from sprue with plastic card fins – all 72 of them! – using the drawings in Appendix II as a guide. The AA–8 Aphids, which are presumably mounted on the outer wing pylons and at the wingtips, although I have yet to see a photograph confirming this, can be taken from the ESCI KAMOV KA–34 HOKUM kit, which has four nicely moulded examples.

All the various aerials, probes, angle-of-attack sensors, Odd-Rods aerials etc. were added using PP Aeroparts where appropriate.

Finishing

The colour scheme applied to the Flanker seen at Paris appears to be overall pale blue with patches of darker blue and mid-grey

Two-seater nosegear with mudguard. (*Photo by Robin Howard*)

Single-seater nosegear – note different style mudguard. (*Photo by Robin Howard*)

FLANKER port intake – note white ESM aerials, metal lower lip and warning stripe. (*Photo by Robin Howard*)

oversprayed on the upper surfaces. My models were completed before the type's Paris appearance and were airbrushed with DBI paints, the undersurfaces Pale Blue (FS35622) and the upper surfaces Gray (FS35562) and Light Gray (FS36492). If I were to try

FLANKER maingear – note locking pin and chocks. (*Photo by Robin Howard*)

and match the Paris scheme I would probably try the Pale Blue overall with the Gray – which is distinctly blue – and add a medium grey.

The vacform Flanker has a dark grey nosecone and dielectric panels, as seen on earlier examples, while the Revell version has these areas in white, again as seen at Paris.

Gloss white, with just a touch of grey added to tone it down, was airbrushed onto the nosecone and fin tips and also onto a piece of clear decal film. This decal film was then cut out to make the panels on the starboard fin leading edge, the upper fuselage spine and either side of the nose below the windscreen. White aerials also appear at the wing-root leading edge, on the intake-mounted fairings and on the end of the tailcone strakes. The Revell decal sheet is very comprehensive with six stars, two sets of red numerals 0–9 in two sizes, all the dielectric panels in dark grey and a host of stencil data. As I wanted to reproduce the Paris machine, I substituted the blue buzz numbers from the spares box. The Sukhoi bureau insignia on the fin was hand-painted and is incorrect, being the earlier style as seen on the SU–25's at Paris. The Flankers had a more stylised logo with the cyrillic script for SU in a triangle, inside a blue outlined white circle – see Fig. 12. The old-style logo is to be found in Hobbycraft's SU–22U Fitter-E kit.

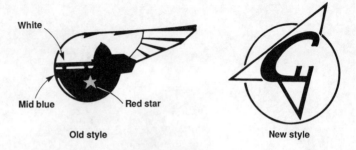

White

Mid blue

Red star

Old style

New style

Fig. 12 Old and new style Sukhoi OKB logo

References

Flight International	26/9/87
	17/6/89
	24/6/89
	2/9/89
	9/9/89
Air International	Aug 1988
	Sep 1989
Air Forces Monthly	Jul 1989
Scale Models International	Oct 1989

21 TUPOLEV TU-28P FIDDLER

TYPE: *TWO-SEAT LONG-RANGE INTERCEPTOR*

ARMAMENT: *4 × AA-5 Ash air-to-air missiles*

The TU-28 FIDDLER must be a candidate for the title of the world's largest fighter. First flown in the late 50s, the Fiddler is now obsolete and is being replaced by the much more capable MiG-31 Foxhound.

Powered by two afterburning Lyulka AL-7F turbojets of approx. 20,000lbs thrust, the Fiddler fulfils the long-range interceptor role along the USSR's northern borders. It is armed with four huge AA-5 Ash missiles, both IR and SARH versions. The nosecone houses a powerful radar, coded Big-Nose by NATO. The design of the TU-28 follows typical Tupolev practice, with the main four-wheel undercarriage bogies retracting into wing trailing edge fairings. Despite its size, the TU-28P carries only two crew members housed in tandem under individual upward opening clamshell canopies, the view from the rear cockpit being very restricted.

Model
There is, to my knowledge, only one 1:72 scale model of the Fiddler available – a vacform by Gerald Elliott of Bristol. While not the best of vacforms, the model measures out well dimensionally and certainly looks like a Fiddler.

The kit consists of two sheets of reasonably stout vacformed plastic, a clear canopy and white-metal parts for the u/c legs, ejection seats, consoles, control column, jetpipe nozzles and wheels. The ejection seats and u/c legs are usable, but the rest are best replaced from the spares box. Indeed, on my example, the wheels (the masters of which come from a source I can't quite place but I know I've seen them before) are badly cast with a step around the circumference where the two halves haven't lined up in the mould. The accompanying instruction sheet has a side profile and half a plan view of the TU-28 and printed silhouettes of the cross sections, from which formers should be cut from plastic card, to strengthen the fuselage. Assembly notes are

Gerald Elliott vacform TU–28P FIDDLER. AA–5 Ash missiles are cut down AA–6 Acrids from FOXBAT kit. (*Model by author; photo by Tim Perry*)

included on the instruction sheet. Decals are not included, but, as the Fiddler seems only to carry a simple scheme of red stars in six positions and a two-digit aircraft number on the nose, this is not an insurmountable problem, given the availability of commercial decals.

Due possibly to the limitations of the moulding process and the dimensions of the packaging, the fuselage is moulded in four pieces – a horizontally split rear with a vertically split forward fuselage. Unfortunately, the split occurs in the worst possible place, just in front of the intakes, which makes filling and rubbing down the joint a difficult task. Intake cones are provided, but no provision is made for the prominent boundary-layer splitter plate.

In order to improve the model's appearance in this area, I removed the forward portion of each intake before cementing the upper and lower fuselage halves together, after first opening up the jetpipes and adding bulkheads cut from plastic card to the patterns provided. This surgery left a gaping hole in the fuselage where the intakes had been removed, which was filled with scrap plastic card. This alteration has the added advantage of allowing the area of the nose joint to be filled and sanded without the intakes getting in the way. Once the joint is made good and smooth, the intakes can be re-cemented in place, after the addition of splitter plates from thin plastic card and the moulded intake cones. The end result of all this surgery is a much better appearance to the whole area of the intakes/fuselage joint. The wings are in upper and lower halves on each side and it is important to get a very thin trailing edge before cementing both halves together. The rear undercarriage pods are moulded in vertically split halves incorporating the pylons, the upper forward portion being moulded integrally with the upper wing. This is another area that requires a lot of cutting and filling to achieve a smooth joint. Cut-outs have to be made in the pods to allow them to butt up against the rear edge of the wing, and copious amounts of filler are used to blend the whole assembly into the wing. Cut-outs are made in the bottom of the pods for the undercarriage bays and a roof and side-walls are added to the box in the bays. When all is satisfactory, the wings can be cemented to the fuselage, after inserting lengths of plastic rod through the fuselage to act as spars.

The vertical tail incorporates a ram-air intake which must be opened up before cementing the two halves together, again ensuring a thin trailing edge. The tailplanes are added next and, after filling all joints and seams, detailing can begin. Jetpipes are

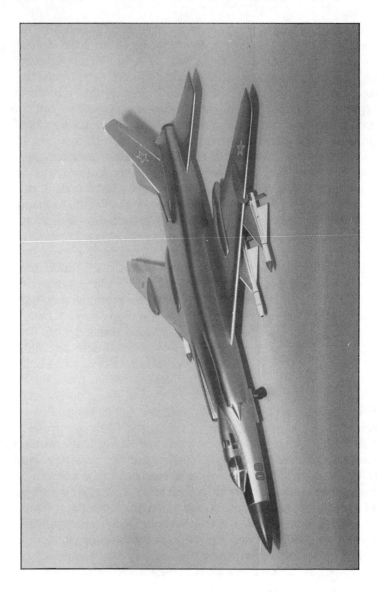

TU–28P FIDDLER. *(Model by author; photo by Tim Perry)*

Size comparison between TU–28P and MiG–21. (Models by author; photo by Tim Perry)

added using suitable diameter plastic tubing, the actual nozzles coming from the spares box. Wing fences are added using the drawing for the shape, as are the outer wing pylons. These latter items are included as mouldings but are best replaced with plastic card suitably sanded to shape. Various protruberances and small intakes can be added from scrap, as can the prominent towel-rail antenna under the forward fuselage. This is well illustrated in some photographs of the real thing but does not appear on the supplied drawing. Cockpit detail can be added to taste but as not much is visible through the canopy, the supplied ejection seats, an instrument panel from scrap and a control column will suffice. The canopy itself is well moulded and needs to be carefully removed from its surround, sanded down to ensure a good fit and cemented in place with super-glue. The model should now be given a thorough wash in soapy water to remove any dust and grease marks and, after masking off the canopy, given a coat of light grey primer. This serves to show up any defects where filler has been used and primes the surface ready for final painting. Once satisfied with the finish, the undercarriage can be added. The white-metal maingear and noselegs can be used, as can the nosewheels, but I needed to replace the mainwheels with items from the spares box. Once painted and cemented in place and the undercarriage doors added, the model is ready for final painting.

I use cling-film wrapped around the undercarriage legs and wheels with tape on the canopy and nosecone to mask them, before spraying with a coat of Humbrol Metalcote Polished Aluminium to provide a surface for a final coat of SNJ Spray Metal. With the paint dry, panel detail can be added by masking off and buffing up with SNJ Powder to achieve varying degrees of shine. The only other areas requiring paint are the nosecone in dark grey or green and a black anti-glare panel in front of the windscreen. Markings consist of white bordered stars in six positions and a two-digit code number on either side of the nose. Canopy framing is from PP Aeroparts Adhesive Silver Foil cut into strips and stuck in place. The four underwing AA–5 Ash missiles will have to be scratch-built using suitable diameter plastic rod, with plastic card fins. I used cut-down AA–6 Acrids from a MiG–25. Colours appear to be white with black or red detail.

References

HCG	p178
Observers	p222

22 YAKOVLEV YAK–28P FIREBAR

TYPE: *TWO-SEAT ALL-WEATHER INTERCEPTOR*

ARMAMENT: *2 × AA–3 Anab IR and SARH AMMs*

Developed from the earlier Yak–25/26/27 family, the transonic Yak–28 features a more sharply swept wing, moved from the mid to the shoulder position and is powered by two Tumansky R–11 turbojets as developed for the MiG–21.

The unusual zero-track bicycle undercarriage has twin main-wheels mounted at the rear of the fuselage and twin nosewheels under the cockpit. The wings are balanced on outriggers mounted in fairings near the wingtips, which extend forward of the wing to form large anti-flutter weights. This arrangement leaves space in the fuselage for fuel or, in the Yak–28's bomber guise – the Brewer – a large internal weapons bay for a tactical nuclear weapon.

The FIREBAR entered IA-PVO service in 1962 and a later version, with longer nosecone and provision for two AA–2 Atoll short-range IR missiles on additional underwing pylons, was reported to have entered front-line service in 1967.

Model
It was this aircraft which started me off on my current craze of modelling Soviet aircraft. When the vacform enterprise of Contrail released a 1:72 scale kit containing both a Firebar and a Brewer, I purchased one straight away. I was fascinated by the unusual layout, with its wing-mounted engine pods, swept-back wings with their strange planform and the odd bicycle undercarriage with wingtip outriggers.

The German vacform company of Airmodel also released a Firebar at about the same time which, I think, featured both long and short-nosed radomes. Other than that I can't say, as I have never seen one, so I will restrict my comments to the more readily available Contrail kit.

This is moulded in thick white plastic and contains enough parts to make the Yak–28P Firebar interceptor *and* the Yak–28B/C

Contrail vacform YAK–28P FIREBAR. Etched brass towbar is a PP Aeroparts 'one-off'. (*Model by author; photo by Tim Perry*)

YAK–28P FIREBAR. Note the unusual configuration. (*Model by author; photo by Tim Perry*)

Brewer tactical fighter-bomber. Alternative parts are given to make different versions of Brewer.

The fuselage is in two vertically split halves with an integrally moulded fin. Openings for the nose and tail wheel bays and the cockpit need to be cut out and boxed-in, for which all the parts are provided. Seats, in white-metal, are supplied but the model will benefit from having them replaced with Aeroclub items. The rest of the cockpit detail is left to the modeller. I added side consoles, instrument panels and a control column and boxed in the area between the pilot and navigator and added a few 'black boxes' – all purely speculative, of course, but enough to make the 'office' look busy.

A bag of parts is supplied which includes, in white-metal, the aforementioned ejection seats plus two Apex missiles (although the drawing correctly shows AA–3 Anabs), four jet-efflux pipes, main and nose undercarriage legs and nose-probe for the Brewer, plus intake cones and wingtip outriggers in injection-moulded plastic. All the parts are usable but require considerable cleaning up. Also in the bag are the mouldings in clear acetate for the tandem Firebar canopy and the Brewer's single-seat canopy and glazed nose, plus decal sheets containing numerous stars, both solid yellow and red-bordered types and two-digit code numbers.

The wings are in upper and lower halves port and starboard which, due to the moulding of the prominent camber on the outer wing panels, cannot be laid flat for sanding, so much scraping is called for to achieve a satisfactory section. Engine nacelles are in upper and lower halves and require the insertion of a bulkhead in the intake before the cones are added. A simple white-metal exhaust ring is added to the rear, to represent the jetpipe. I compromised and detailed one nacelle and left the other unopened, with plastic card discs front and rear to represent the intake and exhaust covers. The detailed nacelle was opened up and a plastic-card bulkhead, with an intake cone from a MiG–21, was fitted to the front, with a jetpipe and exhaust ring added at the rear.

The wings were added to the fuselage with a plastic rod spar for strength. The fitment of the nacelles to the wings called for the application of copious amounts of filler to blend in the joint, while plastic-card wing fences and plastic rod anti-flutter weights were added. The tailplane is a full-span two-part item and fits into a notch cut into the fin.

The vacformed wheels are attached to the white-metal legs and the injection-moulded outriggers are added, making sure that all

Close-up of FIREBAR showing dummy cover over starboard engine intake. Port nacelle is detailed. *(Model by author; photo by Tim Perry)*

Cover over starboard exhaust.

six wheels make contact with the ground. All the undercarriage doors are fabricated from plastic card.

The clear canopy was cut into two parts to depict it in the open position, and required that a portion of the fuselage spine behind the cockpit was removed and added to the clear section for the sake of accuracy. No such surgery is required if the canopy is attached in the closed position.

The model was cleaned up before being airbrushed with Humbrol Metalcote Polished Aluminium (this was before the advent of SNJ Spray Metal) and buffed up to achieve a patchwork effect. Nosecone and fin tip were painted dark grey and the black anti-glare panels in front of the windscreen and on the inner sides of the nacelles were added from solid black decal film. Scratch-built AA–3 Anab missiles were added to home-made pylons, IR on the starboard and SARH to port. Red stars in the usual six positions and a two-digit code in blue were added to complete the model.

References

HCG	p193
Observers	p245
Warplane	No 114

23 YAKOVLEV YAK–38 FORGER-A

TYPE: *SINGLE-SEAT V/STOL SHIPBOARD STRIKE FIGHTER*

ARMAMENT: *4 wing pylons capable of carrying a total load of approx. 7,000lbs*

Following early VTOL experiments with the Yak–36 Freehand in the late 1960s, the Yakovlev OKB developed the much more potent YAK–38 FORGER to operate from the new KIEV class of ASW carriers.

Powered by a combination of two Kolesov lift engines mounted vertically in tandem behind the cockpit and a lift/cruise engine with rotating nozzles in the rear fuselage, thought to be a Lyulka AL–21 turbojet, the Yak–38 has folding wings for carrier stowage. It carries a modest warload, usually consisting of a podded cannon or 57mm rocket pod on the outer pylons and an AA–8 Aphid short-range air-to-air missile on the inners, sufficient for its primary role, which is thought to be reconnaissance and fleet defence against shadowing maritime reconnaissance aircraft.

In its other role of anti-ship strike, the Forger has been observed with an AS–7 Kerry air-to-surface missile mounted on the inner wing pylon.

Model
There are currently two 1:72 scale injection moulded kits of the Forger, by Revell and Hobbycraft.

Hobbycraft's kit consists of 51 parts moulded in light grey plastic with engraved panel detail plus a one-piece clear canopy.

The kit measures up dimensionally against the latest available drawings, except for the fuselage, which is too wide in plan, with a flat top and bottom surface rather than the continuous curve of the original. The whole appearance of the kit is too 'dumpy' – especially around the cockpit and intake areas. This flatness extends to the cockpit canopy which, again, has a flat top to it. Unfortunately, there is little that can be done to correct these errors.

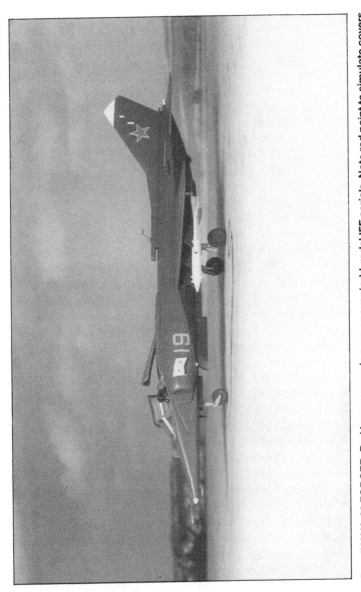

Revell YAK–38 FORGER. Red box on nose is a cover over 'odd-rods' IFF aerials. Note red paint to simulate covers over ram-air intakes and red creep marks on tyres. (*Model by author; photo by Tim Perry*)

Turning to the kit itself – the fuselage is in two vertically split halves with the fin moulded integrally. Two separate inserts represent the lift-engine exhausts and the slatted grill beneath them. Cockpit detail is confined to a rather crude ejection seat, which should be replaced, and a pilot figure. The ram-air intake at the base of the dorsal fillet will benefit from being opened out to a greater diameter.

Wings and tailplanes are single-piece mouldings port and starboard and the intakes, having rather thick lips which need to be thinned down, are separate mouldings. An insert is provided in the top of the fuselage, into which are cemented two discs to represent the lift engines. These look like wheel hubs rather than compressor faces. The intake door which covers these engines is a separate item with moulded-in suction-relief doors and can be cemented in the open or closed position. If the open position is chosen, which seems to be the norm on a parked aircraft, it will require the addition of two retraction jacks made from thin plastic rod – the single item provided being rather thick.

Two strakes are included for fixing to the upper fuselage either side of the intake door. The two swivelling jet nozzles can be made to rotate by carefully cementing them together through the rear fuselage. The undercarriage is neatly moulded with separate main legs and wheels, while the nosegear is a one-piece moulding. Undercarriage doors, lift-engine exhaust doors and ventral strakes are all separate mouldings.

Underwing stores consist of two 3-part rocket pods and two representations of the latest IR short-range missile, the AA–11 Archer. Crudely moulded nose-probe, pitots and dorsal fillet aerial are all best replaced. Detail can be added in the form of an undernose ILS antenna, Odd-Rods IFF aerials at nose and tail, both from PP Aeroparts, static discharge wicks on the flying surfaces and radar warning antennae on the tailcone.

The kit instructions provide for a colour scheme of dark blue upper surfaces and green undersides, which is well illustrated on the cover of *Air International*, June 1981. The simple decal sheet contains six stars, two intake warning triangles, two yellow warning triangles and, curiously, only one yellow warning flash for the upper rear fuselage, plus two AV-MF flags and a pair of two-digit numerals in yellow.

Revell's Forger consists of some 96 parts moulded in grey-blue plastic with fine engraved panel detail, plus a two-part canopy which, although on the thick side, is acceptable. Cockpit detail is confined to a three-part ejection seat, floor and control column.

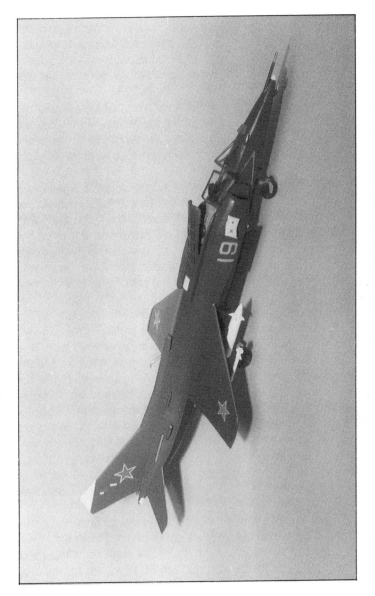

FORGER with armament of two AS–7 Kerry and two AA–8 Aphid missiles. (*Model by author; photo by Tim Perry*)

Each of the two lift engines, which look like oil-drums, are made up from two halves plus a nicely moulded insert for the compressor face. A main lift/cruise engine is supplied, comprising upper and lower halves, a two-part bifurcated jetpipe and a compressor face – all very nice but totally hidden within the fuselage! The lift and main engines, cockpit assembly and lower fuselage lift-engine louvres are cemented in place into the *bottom* half of the *horizontally* split fuselage, before both halves are cemented together.

This unusual arrangement works fine, but it does mean that the joint line runs along the full length of the fuselage mid-way up either side and, on my example at least, the top and bottom halves had to be clamped together fore and aft to overcome a slight 'bowing'.

Wings are almost one-piece either side with just a small insert completing the lower surface, while the horizontal stabilisers are one-piece port and starboard, as is the vertical fin, complete with dorsal fillet and VHF aerial. The ram-air intake in the front of the fillet will need to be opened out for accuracy. The single-piece intake/splitter plates look decidedly undersized when compared with the latest available drawings, but the canopy and windscreen look fine.

Undercarriage legs, wheels and doors are all adequate, as are the two-part rear nozzles and, although no provision is made for them to rotate, they can be cemented in any position. Upper and lower airflow strakes are included as separate parts, as are the four air scoops, pitots, Odd-Rods aerials and sensors, while the lift-engine door has the suction-relief slots opened up. A single actuator is supplied for the door, but a close scrutiny of photographs reveals that the door is raised and lowered by *two* rams, so these will have to be fabricated from sprue. A very comprehensive set of underwing stores is supplied and includes two drop tanks, two AS–7 Kerry anti-ship missiles, four AA–8 Aphid IR AAMs, two bombs and two rocket pods and their associated pylons.

Revell's instruction leaflet manages to name some of the parts, a somewhat parochial but very welcome change from the 'international' style of numbers only. A four-view drawing is included, showing the paint scheme and quoting FS numbers for the blue and grey colours. The drawing indicates that the colour scheme is overall mid-blue, but most references indicate that the Forger sports dark green undersides. The decal sheet contains six stars, the usual two-digit codes in yellow, two yellow warning arrows with legible cyrillic script on them, four tiny white aerial panels for the fin, two AV-MF flags and two sets of intake warning triangles – the latter are solid red rather than the more normal chevrons.

All in all, this is a good kit which is more refined and delicate than the Hobbycraft offering, with a better canopy and a more rounded fuselage, although I still have reservations about the intakes.

References

HCG	p196
Air International	Jun 1981
(Front cover colour picture)	
Air International	Aug 1986
(Six page article)	

APPENDIX I
USEFUL NAMES AND ADDRESSES

Most of the models featured in this book will be available from the major model shops, but some of the vacforms and certainly some of the accessories can only be obtained through the specialist mail-order hobby shops. In case of difficulty, listed here are the names and addresses of some of the smaller manufacturers.

Aeroclub
5 Silverwood Avenue
Ravenshead
Notts, UK
NG15 9BU

Contrail
Sutcliffe Productions
Westcombe
Shepton Mallet
Somerset, UK
BA4 6RA

Gerald Elliot
76 Station Rd
Filton
Bristol, UK
BS12 7JJ

PP Aeroparts
Unit 12
Station Rd Workshops
Kingswood
Bristol, UK
BS15 4PR

Planes Vacforms
(Via PP Aeroparts)

Scale Cast
43 Hawksley Ave
Chesterfield
Derby, UK
S40 4TJ

International Plastic
Modelling Society (UK)
Liaison Officer
Steve Di Nucci
259 Stockwood Lane
Stockwood, Bristol
Avon, BS14 8NR

IPMS UK – SOVIET SPECIAL
INTEREST GROUP (SIG)
Gordon Millar
6 Petworth Close
Frimley
Surrey
GU16 5XS

SNJ Spray Metal
SNJ Model Products
Sacremento
California
USA

Eastern Bloc Modellers
Guild
PO Box 15553
New Orleans
LA 70175–5553
USA

Red Bear
30 Stride Avenue
Copnor
Portsmouth
Hants
PO3 6HL

APPENDIX II
SOVIET AIR-TO-AIR MISSILES
1:72 SCALE

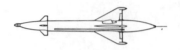

K–51 AA–1 ALKALI

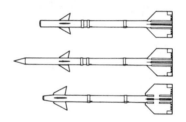

K–13 AA2 ATOLL

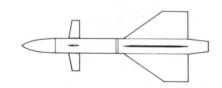

AA–3 ANAB

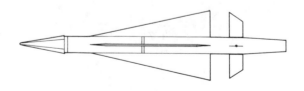

AA–5 ASH

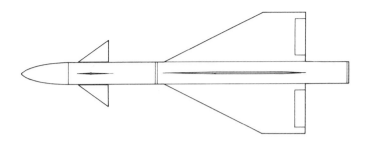

AA–6 ACRID

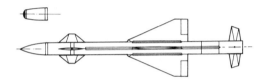

R–23 AA–7 APEX

R–60 AA–8 APHID

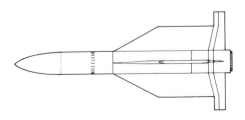

AA–9 AMOS

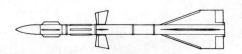

R–27 AA–10 ALAMO

R–73 AA–11 ARCHER